Case of a Lifetime

Case of a Lifetime

A Criminal Defense Lawyer's Story

Abbe Smith

palgrave
macmillan

First published in 2008 by PALGRAVE MACMILLAN® in the US-a
division of St. Martin's Press LLC, 175 Fifth Avenue, New York, NY
10010.

Where this book is distributed in the UK, Europe and the rest of the
world, this is by Palgrave Macmillan, a division of Macmillan
Publishers Limited, registered in England, company number 785998, of
Houndmills, Basingstoke, Hampshire RG21 6XS.

Palgrave Macmillan is the global academic imprint of the above
companies and has companies and representatives throughout the
world.

Palgrave® and Macmillan® are registered trademarks in the United
States, the United Kingdom, Europe and other countries.

ISBN-13: 978–0–230–60528–2
ISBN-10: 0–230–60528–1

Library of Congress Cataloging-in-Publication Data
Smith, Abbe.
    Case of a lifetime : a criminal defense lawyer's story / Abbe Smith.
        p.   cm.
    Includes bibliographical references and index.
    ISBN 0–230–60528–1
    1. Smith, Abbe.   2. Jarrett, Patsy Charlene Kelly, 1951–   3. Trials
(Murder)—New York (State)—Utica.   4. Defense (Criminal
procedure)—New York (State)—Utica.   5. Attorney and client—
United States.   6. Legal ethics—United States.   I. Title.
KF224.J36S65   2008
345.747'6202523—dc22

                                                                2007052444

A catalogue record of the book is available from the British Library.

Design by Letra Libre

First edition: August 2008
10 9 8 7 6 5 4 3 2 1
Printed in the United States of America.

For Sally Greenberg,

Joseph Nathan Smith Greenberg,

and, of course,

Patsy Kelly Jarrett

"[S]imply by the nature of the work, every lawyer gets at least one case in his lifetime that affects him personally. This one's mine, I guess."

Atticus Finch, in Harper Lee's *To Kill a Mockingbird*

Contents

Case of a Lifetime

Prologue

Truth is a complicated and elusive matter in criminal defense. More often than not, it is also in the eye of the beholder. One person maintains one version of events while another offers a very different account. Each is certain of what happened and can point to facts that support their truth. But facts can be unruly. Judges and juries are sometimes called "fact-finders," yet there is no science to finding facts. Even seemingly incontrovertible facts—a bloody trail, presence at a crime scene, an admission of guilt—can be deceptive. Things are not always what they seem.

If the truth lies somewhere between objective reality and subjective experience, it is not always easy to pinpoint. There is no bright line between what really happened and what might have. The question of guilt and innocence is no simpler. Although lawyers, judges, and juries are supposed to be able to make these judgments, even the conscientious can get it wrong. Important legal protections, like the presumption of innocence and the requirement that the government prove its case beyond a reasonable doubt, are not foolproof. As of 2008, more than 200 U.S. prisoners have been exonerated by DNA evidence. Most were locked up for years before being cleared.

These 200-plus cases are likely the tip of the iceberg. With mistaken identification a leading cause of wrongful convictions and eyewitness testimony a common feature in criminal trials, it is impossible to say how many people are behind bars for crimes they didn't commit. When mistakes happen, DNA evidence is available in only a fraction of cases to set things right. Moreover, notwithstanding the media attention that accompanies exonerations or the sudden popularity of Innocence Projects here and abroad, there is tremendous resistance to the idea that a convicted prisoner *didn't do it.*

I was in my second year of law school when I met Patsy Kelly Jarrett. She said her friends called her Kelly, not Patsy. She had come to despise the name Patsy because it summed up too precisely what had happened to her. She was a fool, a chump. She had played the patsy in the summer of 1973—her first and last adult summer vacation—and had been paying for it ever since.

It was early autumn 1980 when we shook hands and sat together for the first time in the visiting room of the Bedford Hills Correctional Facility in Westchester County, New York. I had just turned 24, and Kelly was about to turn 29. I hadn't known what to expect when I traveled to the prison that morning. Although there were press clippings about Kelly's case in the file, there were no photographs. I had a sense of her from her letters—from what she had written and her careful penmanship—but I didn't have a picture of her in my head. Now here she was: a pretty tomboy with a fresh-scrubbed look and a soft southern accent.

Her warmth was reassuring. She was glad to see me. She didn't seem to mind that I was not a lawyer, only partway through law school, and younger than she was. Maybe she had no choice but to be gracious: She needed help, had no money to pay for it, and the services provided by the law school clinic were free. She asked about the train ride from the city to Bedford Hills. She wondered whether this was my first trip.

It was. I had been to a few other prisons and jails. As a high school student in suburban Chicago, I had toured the Cook County Jail with my sociology class. When the group got to the bakery, one of the inmates working there called out to us, asking whether anyone wanted a loaf of bread. The other students laughed, but I said, "Sure." When he tossed me a fresh loaf, I felt honored. My mother did not share my enthusiasm and refused to serve the "prison bread" at dinner.

That first jail visit touched something in me. Although I was slightly embarrassed to be part of a field trip—a bunch of mostly white kids gawking at the mostly black prisoners like we were at the zoo—I felt oddly at home. Many of the prisoners were not much older than we were. They didn't seem to mind our trooping through. They were friendly. Maybe we were as much a curiosity to them as they were to us.

Besides my high school experience, the summer before I met Kelly I had worked in the criminal division of the legal aid office in New Haven, Connecticut. Part of the job was meeting with clients at the local city jail and state prison. I liked working with prisoners. I felt a kinship.

I had been eager to see Bedford Hills, a famous women's prison. It wasn't famous in the way of Attica with its riots, Alcatraz with its Birdman, Angola with its rodeo, or neighboring Sing Sing with Jimmy Cagney; men's prisons have a deeper foothold in the popular culture. But Bedford had its share of notorious inmates. It was the only maximum-security prison for women in New York, and there were many stories behind its walls.

The visiting room where I met Kelly that first day had the look and feel of a 1960s-style cafeteria. A couple dozen nondescript tables with vaguely matching chrome-legged plastic chairs were arbitrarily arranged in a large room. The chairs were probably designed for stacking, not sitting: the smooth, hard plastic made you feel like you were about to slide off. Vending machines lined one wall. But since inmates are not allowed to carry money, the candy, snacks, and sodas were available only if the visitor did the buying. Experienced prison visitors always arrive with a pocketful of change.

On the far end of the visiting room sat the oddly welcoming Children's Center. Designed to help women preserve family ties by encouraging visits from their children, the center was a bright and friendly place removed from the intensity of the main visiting room. Entire lifetimes occurred in this room—people wept and laughed, had fallings out and reconciliations, reminisced about the past and despaired for the future. The Children's Center was an entirely separate, protected space. From inside, it looked like any other daycare center. It had a rocking horse, easel, children's table and chair set, toys, board games, and *Sesame Street* posters. The mothers and children who visited there could almost forget they were in a prison. The guard station and the electronically locked gate from which the women emerged for visits were on the opposite end of the room. The children were far enough away for the sound of metal doors creaking open and slamming shut to be muted. But the distance didn't stop children from howling and clinging to their mothers' legs when the visit was over and the women went back through to the other side.

Kelly seemed both old and young to me on that first visit. Nothing ages a person like prison, and she had already spent the better part of her 20s there. But she also had a youthful innocence about her. By any estimation of human nature, she should have lost that part of herself when, in 1976, she was taken from her home near High Point, North Carolina, and jailed in a distant town in upstate New York, perhaps never to return, charged with a crime she always said she did not commit.

I had read the trial transcript to prepare for the meeting so I knew enough to have a conversation about the case. At trial, the prosecution maintained that Kelly, who had traveled to Utica, New York, in the summer of 1973, had helped her traveling companion rob and murder a 17-year-old gas station attendant named Paul David Hatch in the nearby town of Sherrill. The companion was a man named Billy Ronald Kelly—no relation, but the shared name would serve to further tie the two together. Kelly was not alleged to have actually committed the robbery or murder. She was accused of being an accomplice: the lookout or getaway driver. At trial, a witness who came through the Seaway gas station shortly after the crime testified that he saw Kelly behind the wheel of a car there. The car was said to match the one Kelly owned, the same car in which she and Billy Ronald had driven north.

The positive identification of Kelly at trial was a first for the witness. When initially questioned by the police, he said that he did not see the driver's face and could not say for sure whether it was a man or a woman. He could not describe the driver's age, build, clothing, speech, or manner. The witness had never seen the person before and had only gotten a glance. There had been no reason to pay further attention.

But the witness did pay attention to the man who pumped his gas that day. He got a good, close look at the man. He had never seen this man at the station before, and there was something peculiar about him. He seemed nervous making conversation and had trouble making change, even though he had a large wad of cash jammed in his pocket. Based on his observations, the witness provided the police with a detailed description of the man and assisted a police artist in creating a composite sketch.

It turned out that Billy Ronald had posed as the gas station attendant after killing the real attendant and making off with $279. When the police discovered the victim's bound and gagged body in a back room, his throat cut nearly to the point of decapitation, they also found Billy Ronald's fingerprints. Adhesive tape, a surface from which prints are easily lifted, had been used to bind the victim's feet and hands.

It took the police more than two years to match the prints to Billy Ronald. Initially they had focused on local suspects, and Billy Ronald was not from around there. The police would later learn that killing and robbing were not unusual for Billy Ronald. Not long after he left New York, he was arrested and convicted of killing and robbing a gas station attendant outside of Danville, Virginia, just north of the North Carolina border. By the time he was tried in New York, Billy Ronald was already serving a 35-year sentence.

When the police paid a visit to the witness some two and a half years after the crime, he was able to select a photograph of Billy Ronald as the man who had pumped gas for him at the Seaway station. He immediately signed the back of Billy Ronald's picture, saying this was the man he'd seen. He told the police he was sure.

The case against Kelly was not nearly as strong. It was a "one-witness identification case," with no corroboration to speak of. In contrast to the witness's immediate identification of Billy Ronald's photograph, when he was shown photos for the driver—females only—he picked out two, saying they both looked like the person in the car. At two different pretrial proceedings, the witness continued to express uncertainty about the gender of the second person he had seen at the station. He also expressed doubt about the photograph of Kelly, saying only that she might have been the driver. Though Kelly was present at one of the proceedings, the witness failed to identify her in court.

As I read the transcript, it was hard not to be struck by the fact that the only time the witness positively identified Kelly was at trial. Even though he had never done so before, at trial he made his identification with confidence and certainty. It did not trouble the witness—nor did it trouble the jury—that three and a half years had passed since he had glanced at another car in a gas station. It did not trouble the witness—nor did it trouble the jury—that a witness who could not even describe the person he saw, and who had never before made a positive identification, now had no doubt.

The prosecution claimed that the two defendants were partners: partners in crime and in life. Witnesses testified that the two traveled north together, stayed overnight in the same room while on the road, rented a room together in Utica, spent time at the same bar, and shared the use of Kelly's car. Recognizing the danger of guilt by association for Kelly, her court-appointed lawyer had asked for separate trials. The trial judge denied the motion.

Kelly testified at trial. She denied being at the Seaway station on August 11, 1973, denied any knowledge of what happened there, and said she was innocent.

The jury was out for two days. I knew from Kelly's letters that the verdict came as a shock. When the jury found her guilty, she thought there had been some kind of mistake, that the jury had confused Billy Ronald's verdict with her own. This could not be what the jury had decided. Kelly believed in the system. She believed in the law. She had been certain that she would be found not guilty because she was *not guilty*.

A few weeks later she was sentenced to life in prison.

As I sat with her in the prison that first day, more than three years after her trial, I could feel her continuing disbelief. She still could not believe that she had been convicted of murder. She could hardly say the word. She said that people at the prison kept saying that in time she would "adjust." She just shook her head. "How am I supposed to adjust?" she wanted to know. She said she would be grateful for any help I could offer.

It is now more than 25 years later. Kelly served 28–1/2 years in prison before she was finally released on June 13, 2005. At the time of her release, she was one of the longest-serving women in the New York prison system.

During the time she was in prison, both of Kelly's parents died. Before her father died, he wrote to Governor George Pataki that his only wish in the world was to see "his girl" again. He never got a reply. When Kelly finally emerged from prison, the only family she had left was an elderly uncle and her younger brother, now middle aged. Both are from the South and couldn't afford to visit her in New York. Barely out of his teens when his sister was tried and convicted, Kelly's brother had a hard time with her incarceration and kept away during most of it.

Many people passed through Bedford Hills during Kelly's time there, some more than once. The first two digits of Kelly's prison number, 77-G–0098—marked on every letter she sent and received, typed on every prison document that bore her name, sewn above the left breast pocket on her industrial-green prison shirt—served as a constant reminder of the year she arrived and the passage of time since then. Kelly spent her 20s, 30s, and 40s in prison. She was 53 years old when she got out.

Kelly managed to make a life for herself behind bars. She made some friends there. When she refers to another prisoner, she often says, "We grew up together." She marvels at the women who left prison while she remained there, only to return with new offenses. She thinks that returning to prison must be even worse than being sent there the first time around. Kelly knows that life on the outside is hard for many women—family disagreements, financial problems, the lack of decent-paying jobs, and the temptation of drugs and alcohol can be overwhelming. But she also knows that now that she is finally out, she will never return. At least not as a prisoner.

As for me, I have been a criminal lawyer since graduating from law school in 1982. First I was a public defender, working to ensure that what happened to Kelly did not happen to anyone else. Then I became a clinical law professor, teaching students about people like Kelly who get caught up in the system. Over the years, I have represented thousands of clients in several different states and the District of Columbia. I have seen the system up close and know it well. Like many criminal lawyers, I both believe in the system and am wary of it.

Kelly's case, my very first, remains the most haunting miscarriage of justice I have ever encountered. In 1973 she took up with a man she had known for less than a year who turned out to be a killer. Unsuspecting by nature, she never imagined that her traveling companion was leading a double life—that beneath Billy Ronald's mild-mannered exterior lay a murderer.

No doubt Billy Ronald was drawn to Kelly's naiveté. It made for an easy cover.

Kelly has never wavered in her assertion of innocence. Even though she is now out of prison, she would give anything to prove she was not at the Seaway gas station that August afternoon and had nothing to do with the terrible events that occurred there. She would give anything to prove her innocence. Unfortunately, no such proof exists. Although many wrongfully convicted prisoners have been vindicated thanks to technology that matches crime-scene DNA to the perpetrator's DNA, this technology never had anything to offer Kelly. Because she was alleged to be no more than an accomplice, the absence of her DNA at the scene of the crime is not exonerating.

This is the story of Patsy Kelly Jarrett, a woman failed by the system. She committed no crime but spent decades in prison. She remains a convicted murderer today. Though many believe her to be innocent, she has no hope for vindication. She expects to be under the supervision of the New York Parole Board for the rest of her life.

I tried for years to obtain the justice she wanted but managed only to help secure her release on parole. I confess that this book was partly born of my own sense of failure. No matter how hard I worked, the righteousness of the cause, and the resources at my disposal, an innocent person served nearly 30 years in prison.

I am telling Kelly's story with her encouragement. She knows that she is not alone in her plight—there are many other wrongly convicted prisoners lost in the system—and some good might come of the telling. I know, too, that I'm not the only lawyer who has tried and failed to right a wrong. Perhaps the telling will resonate with others—lawyers, journalists, prison advocates, family members—who have tried to undo an injustice and failed.

In telling Kelly's story I will also tell my own.

Chapter 1

Innocence

P atsy Charlene Kelly Jarrett was born on November 7, 1951, in Washington, D.C. The eldest of two children born to Rufus Kelly, a former World War II army sergeant turned butcher and grocer, and Jean Mildred Kelly, a secretary nearly 20 years her husband's junior, Kelly was raised in Trinity, North Carolina, a small town located outside of High Point.

Kelly's parents divorced when she was 12. When her mother moved back to Washington for a government job, Kelly and her 6-year-old brother, Eddie, stayed with their father. It was an unusual arrangement in the early 1960s, but Jean, who struggled with alcoholism and depression, saw that the kids were better off with their father.

Kelly was happy to stay with her father. Although he had wanted his firstborn to be a boy—he was so certain Kelly would be a boy he had only a male name picked out—Rufus was crazy about his girl from the moment he laid eyes on her. When Kelly cast off dresses and dolls for a pair of overalls and a baseball glove, he didn't mind. He liked his daughter's pluck. If Kelly was happy playing ball with the neighborhood boys, and helping out at the Circle J (the small grille and grocery store her father co-owned), then he was happy, too. Rufus reckoned it was Kelly's life, not his, and he couldn't live it for her.

Kelly felt at ease with her father too. When, as a teenager, she told him that she was a lesbian, he didn't seem surprised. He told his daughter that being gay in the small-town South wouldn't be an easy life, but he would always be in her corner.

Growing up, Kelly's family lived next to a small farm. She worked there in exchange for boarding privileges for her family's two horses, feeding, cleaning, and exercising the horses and mucking out their stalls. From a young age it was clear that Kelly was a natural horsewoman. By the time she was 12 she could break and train a horse. She often rode at horse shows and parades. In addition to horses, Kelly's family had dogs: a collie, a Labrador retriever, and a favorite cocker spaniel mix named "Jep"—for Jean, Eddie, and Patsy. Kelly spent a lot of time training Jep, who could shake hands, roll over, and jump through hoops like a circus dog. At the end of the day, Jep would sleep curled up in Kelly's legs.

When Kelly was in her early teens, her father remarried. After his second wife died, he married again. Between the two stepmothers, Rufus had three more children, all girls. Though Kelly and her father remained close, there was tension between her and the stepmothers. This was especially so with the second stepmother, who acted like she didn't want Kelly and Eddie around. This stepmother was also uncomfortable with Kelly's sexual orientation and declared that she wouldn't "accept it." She worried that Kelly's lesbianism was a corrupting influence on her own young daughters. She set about remaking Kelly by giving her feminine clothing—skirts, dresses, a flowered blouse. She was always after Rufus to treat Kelly more like a *girl*.

Kelly enjoyed school and was well liked by teachers and peers. Though she wasn't studious—she preferred the outdoors to the classroom—she was a good enough student. Her favorite and best subject was gym, and she thought about becoming a PE teacher until she realized how much schooling was involved. She played all the team sports for girls: basketball, volleyball, and softball. Her best sport was softball. Her quick glove and good arm made her an ideal infielder.

Kelly had a small circle of close friends and a best friend named Terry. When she wasn't playing sports or working, Kelly was often at Terry's house, where she was considered a member of the family. They were not in the "cool crowd"—football players and cheerleaders, prom kings and queens—but they weren't in the tough crowd either. They stayed away from kids who smoked, drank, or got picked up by the police. Though Kelly grew up in tobacco country, she believed smoking was unhealthy long before government-mandated warnings. She didn't drink because she didn't like the taste of alcohol. She had no interest whatsoever in drugs.

Kelly was no goody-two-shoes, but she *was* good. She couldn't help herself; that's who she was. She was the girl next door, the grocer's daughter, that nice kid who hung out at the stables and the ball field. There was something wholesome about her.

Kelly had worked her whole life, ever since she was old enough to stamp prices at her dad's store. From the time she graduated from high school in 1968 until she was arrested in 1976, Kelly was steadily employed. Aside from working at the store, she worked at several local factories that made anvils, furniture parts, plastic objects, and elastic products. She worked in the textile mills, at a local stable, and in a veterinarian's clinic. She continued to live in Trinity after graduation, eschewing the big-city life of High Point or Winston-Salem because she wanted to be close to her dad, brother, and childhood friends. Trinity was home.

Kelly knew that she liked girls early on. It wasn't the kind of thing anyone talked about, but she didn't feel ashamed of her feelings either. As soon as she could name it, she called herself a lesbian. She never had any doubt about her sexual orientation and considered herself gay through and through. To her father's surprise and stepmother's delight, not long after high school graduation, Kelly married a man named Johnny Jarrett. She did it on a lark—to fit into small-town life, to move out of her stepmother's house, and because Johnny was eager. But it was not a marriage in any true sense. Johnny and Kelly both considered themselves gay, and they married as a way of joining forces. The marriage was short-lived. When Johnny began to have feelings that Kelly didn't share, she put an end to it. She never bothered to change her name back after the divorce.

Patsy Kelly Jarrett and Billy Ronald Kelly met in the fall of 1972, when they were working at the same High Point textile mill. They were introduced by mutual friends who knew they were both gay. High Point was not exactly a gay mecca in the early 1970s, but there was a fledgling community and a local gay bar. As in many towns, there was a not-so-secret club for sexual outsiders—men who liked men, women who liked women, those who "went both ways"—most of whom led outwardly conventional lives.

The fact that Kelly and Billy Ronald were both gay, worked at the same place, and had friends in common created a bond. It didn't matter that Kelly didn't really know Billy Ronald. Familiarity, recognition, a sense of *sameness* can be comforting. As young, gay southerners, Kelly and Billy Ronald took comfort in each other. They felt like family.

When Billy Ronald suggested they take a trip to New York in the summer of 1973, Kelly didn't think twice.

They quit their jobs and headed north in Kelly's car, a 1970 metallic blue, two-door Plymouth Road Runner. Kelly was proud of that car. It was a "muscle car"—built to be feisty, fast, with few frills: the perfect car for a working-class tomboy. When Kelly first saw it, on the used car lot a few months before the Utica trip, she just had to have it. She traded in her old Ford Mustang, put some money down, and came away with a car James Dean would've been proud to own: a late-model, four-on-the-floor Road Runner, with silver-slotted mag wheels, deep-set grille and headlights, and a slightly jacked up rear.

Kelly liked the look of the car and loved the way it drove. She kept it clean, inside and out, even polishing the wheels. She was fastidious that way. It made perfect sense that she and Billy Ronald would use her Road Runner on the trip north. He wasn't driving anything nearly as nice.

She and Billy Ronald made the trip to Utica in a couple of days, staying with some people he knew along the way. They seemed glad to see Billy Ronald, and welcomed Kelly. The trip north was pleasant and uneventful.

In Utica, Kelly and Billy Ronald made themselves part of the gay community. Like High Point, Utica was hardly a popular gay destination. Still, there was a local gay bar, the Hub, and a bartender named Gerri. Kelly immediately developed a crush on her, and, before long, they became lovers. Kelly spent most of her days with Gerri and her nights at the Hub. On weekends, she hung out with the Angels, a local women's softball team, and watched their games. Gerri played shortstop for the Angels, and Kelly was friendly with some of the other players. Kelly would have liked to have joined the team herself, but it was too late in the season.

Meanwhile, Billy Ronald found work as a laborer, working construction at a nearby apartment complex. This was the arrangement between him and Kelly: He would get a job and pay for their lodging in exchange for the use of Kelly's car. Kelly would rely on savings for her other expenses. This worked for both of them. It was easier for a man to find a decent-paying job, and Kelly was happy to be on vacation for a few weeks. Billy Ronald was the kind of guy who liked to have a wad of cash in his pocket. Kelly did fine on less.

Their time in Utica came to an end in mid-August when Kelly ran out of money. That had pretty much been the plan. Summer was winding down, and it was time for her and Billy Ronald to go home. She called her father and he wired her $40 for the trip back. She hugged her softball friends good-bye, bid a tearful farewell to her summer love, and headed south.

Back in Trinity, she resumed her old life. She found work, hung out at the stables, played ball, spent time with family and friends, and frequented the local gay bar. She and Billy Ronald parted ways when they got home. During their time in Utica and especially on the ride back home, Kelly saw some things in Billy Ronald she didn't like. He was not who she thought he was.

Two and a half years later, there was a knock on the door of Kelly's rented mobile home. Two police officers wanted to know where she was on August 11, 1973, at around 1:00 P.M. She told them she was in Utica, New York, but she couldn't be sure exactly where she was on that particular day, at that particular time. It was more than two years ago and nothing stood out. The officers showed her a picture of a gas station and asked her whether she had ever been there. She said she may have bought gas there once. It looked familiar.

They told her she was wanted for the murder and robbery of 17-year-old Paul David Hatch.

The annals of legal scholarship are replete with discussions of— and justifications for—representing the guilty. This is the most frequently asked question about criminal defense. Every criminal defense lawyer invariably confronts the "Question": *How can you defend people you know to be guilty?*[1]

The Question—which is usually asked at cocktail parties when the target of the query has a drink in hand and his or her guard down—can be posed by the genuinely perplexed as well as the hardened heckler. The person questioned has heard it many times before and, if gracious, will try not to appear peevish. He or she might offer any number of standard replies—about the adversary system requiring competent counsel on both sides, the critical role of the defense lawyer in ensuring access to justice, the importance of checking official power and of protecting the rights of the guilty as well as the innocent.

One commentator who at first dismisses the Question as a matter of utter unimportance later suggests that devoting one's career to defending the guilty might simply be a matter of "taste." Likening defenders to doctors who specialize in disorders of the colon, rectum, and anus, he says, "It is important to remember that, for one reason or another, criminal lawyers want to defend criminal defendants. Their taste may be as baffling to us as is the proctologist's, but we need both and should not try to dissuade either from pursuing his or her profession."[2]

George Sharswood, a prominent nineteenth-century Philadelphia lawyer who wrote an influential essay on lawyers' ethics, was one of the first to put forward a principled argument for defending the guilty. Sharswood argued that lawyers must zealously represent the innocent and guilty alike lest they usurp the function of the fact-finder. It is for judges and juries to judge the accused; lawyers should *represent* them.[3]

Charles Curtis, a leading twentieth-century Boston lawyer who also wrote an important article on lawyers' ethics, likened the criminal lawyer representing a guilty client to the civil lawyer who takes on a "bad" or unpopular case. He argued that both serve the system.[4]

Some commentators discuss the need to defend the guilty for symbolic reasons: to show that everyone, no matter the allegation, has the right to their day in court. This ideal can be met only through competent counsel. When the worst, most wicked criminal—Oklahoma City bomber Timothy McVeigh, Washington, D.C., area sniper John Muhammed—receives proper counsel and a fair trial, we can rest assured that the system is working.

One of the most famous proponents of the importance of representing the guilty and unpopular was the second President of the United States, John Adams. Adams was a 34-year-old lawyer when eight British soldiers opened fire on a crowd of colonials, killing five. There was enormous public outcry against the killings, which became known as the Boston Massacre, and the soldiers and their captain were charged with murder. While others hesitated, Adams stepped forward to defend the redcoats. He believed that "no man in a free country should be denied the right to counsel and a fair trial."⁵ Adams said, "[I]f by supporting the rights of mankind, and of invincible truth, I shall contribute to save from the agonies of death one unfortunate victim of tyranny, or of ignorance, equally fatal, his blessings and years of transport will be sufficient consolation to me for the contempt of all mankind."⁶

Adams was largely successful in his defense of the soldiers. By depicting the colonials as an angry, threatening mob against which the soldiers acted in self-defense, he obtained acquittals for the captain and six of the eight soldiers. The two remaining soldiers were found guilty of manslaughter for which they were branded on their thumbs. Later in life Adams described the case as "the most exhausting" he ever undertook, but also "one of the most gallant, generous, manly, and disinterested actions of [his] whole life."⁷

Other commentators cite pragmatic reasons for defending the guilty. Although most people accused of crime are usually guilty of something, defense lawyers serve an important testing function. If nothing else, they ensure the government's evidence is trustworthy enough to support a conviction by probing and challenging it. They make sure the guilty are convicted of what they actually did as a matter of fact and law, an important safeguard against over-charging or wrongful charging. Criminal defenders also ensure that the constitutional rights of the accused are protected and that police, prosecutors, and judges comply with the law.⁸

Prominent legal ethics scholar Monroe Freedman has long argued that zealous advocacy on behalf of the guilty and nonguilty alike is in keeping with the basic principles underlying the Bill of Rights.⁹ A lawyer who defends the accused embraces the dignity and humanity of the individual in the face of a powerful and sometimes oppressive system. Zealous defenders also make sure that the least of us—the detested and the destitute—have the same rights and privileges as anyone. As New York public defender Martin Erdmann stated in a 1971 *Life* magazine article that became an instant criminal defense classic: "I'm concerned with seeing that every client gets as good representation as he could if he had $200,000. I don't want him to get screwed just because there wasn't anyone around to see that he's not getting screwed."[10]

Renowned Australian defense lawyer Frank Galbally was asked the Question many times during his long career. He had a particularly thoughtful answer:

> The rule of law is a fundamental requirement of a civilised state. Its development has taken many centuries. Its origin and preservation owe a great deal to the courage and independence of advocates who have fought for its recognition regardless of the consequences. . . . [W]ithout the rule of law and the freedom of advocates to protect it, democracy is void of meaning, and the liberty of individuals is in jeopardy at the hands of arbitrary power. . . .
>
> Clients come to me to represent them and take upon my shoulders their cause, not the Crown's or the public's or anyone else's. In doing so they do not ask for my judgement of their cause or for me to turn them into witnesses against themselves, for I am neither a prosecutor nor a judge. If I assume either role I become a grave threat, not only to my clients but also to the interests of justice and the freedom of the individual.[11]

Clarence Darrow, whose name is synonymous with defending unpopular causes in this country, gave a more personal answer. For Darrow, defending the accused, whether innocent or guilty, reflected a passionate engagement in life itself: "Strange as it may seem I grew to like to defend men and women charged with crime. It soon came to be something more than winning or losing a case. . . . [It] meant more than the quibbling with lawyers and juries, to get or keep money for a client so that I could take part of what I won or saved for him: I was dealing with life, with its hopes and fears, its aspirations and despairs."[12]

According to Stanford law professor Barbara Babcock, the Question is actually three different questions, each of which requires its own answer: *How* can you represent the guilty (how can you reconcile the moral dilemmas that such work entails); how can *you* represent the guilty (why you, with your elite education and endless professional opportunities); and how can you *represent* the guilty (how far will you go on behalf of such clients)?[13]

There are no right answers to the Question or related questions. The skeptic will not be convinced no matter how clever the reply. The best answers inevitably reflect the personality, philosophy, and experience of the individual lawyer. Still, fascination with the Question persists.

Within the scholarly literature, there is often little more than a comment about the related issue of defending the innocent. For some reason, scholars and commentators have shown little interest in this question.

Yet plenty of popular literature and film is built on the drama of a wrongful or questionable accusation. From a narrative perspective, there is nothing better than a story about an innocent person caught up in the system. There seems to be a particular American fascination with these stories.[14]

But these stories seldom explore the peculiar burden innocence places on the professional. The lawyer representing an innocent—whether Atticus Finch or Perry Mason—appears calm and implacable, no matter how unjust the prosecution.

Perhaps the lack of scholarly attention to defending the innocent reflects the fact that most people regard such work as self-evidently righteous. What more do we need to know about lawyers who defend the innocent? We appreciate and admire these lawyers: They're the best of the breed. Even people who generally don't like lawyers like these lawyers. As Holden Caulfield says in *The Catcher in the Rye:*

> "Lawyers are all right, I guess—but it doesn't appeal to me. . . . I mean they're all right if they go around saving innocent guys' lives all the time, and like that, but you don't do that kind of stuff if you're a lawyer. All you do is make a lot of dough and play golf and play bridge and buy cars and drink Martinis and look like a hot-shot. How would you know you weren't being a phony? The trouble is, you wouldn't."[15]

Perhaps we don't wonder about what it's like to defend an innocent because we believe the system does it. Under our legal system, the guilty receive all kinds of protections so that the innocent will be ferreted out, identified, and vindicated. Most people believe the system works, and if lawyers do their job properly, the truly innocent will prevail. Most believe that if a mistake happens, the accused was probably guilty anyway; if not, they can appeal. Most people, including legal scholars, seem to think that if lawyers do what they're supposed to do and place their faith in the system, there is no particular challenge to representing the innocent.

The problem is that the system is far from perfect. And it's not just because witnesses, jurors, and judges make mistakes. A recent study of 124 exonerations of death row inmates in the United States found that two-thirds of wrongful convictions resulted from intentional misconduct by police and prosecutors. The misconduct included putting lying witnesses on the stand, failing to disclose facts favorable to the defense, and manufacturing or destroying evidence. Much of the misconduct was well intentioned: Police and prosecutors believed the accused was guilty of a heinous crime and wanted to ensure a conviction. As the study shows, these motivations are often a recipe for disaster.[16]

Sometimes the system fails. Even good and diligent lawyers fail. Too often—especially when the stakes are high—it's not a fair fight.

Most criminal lawyers agree that nothing is more difficult than defending the innocent. As Professor Babcock notes: "Those rare trials of a defendant the lawyer truly believes to be innocent . . . are grueling and frightening experiences."[17]

⌒

John Scholl, a local Utica lawyer, was appointed to represent Kelly. Scholl had a small general practice with another lawyer but regularly accepted criminal appointments. He didn't distinguish between his private cases and appointed ones. He understood that his professional obligations were the same whether a client paid him or the county did. Besides, Scholl was not very good at the financial part of law practice. His partner complained that he never wanted to charge anyone.

Scholl was in his mid-40s when he took on Kelly's case. Married with three children, he was known as a hardworking, conscientious attorney. A large man, with a full head of wavy hair and a handsome Irish face, Scholl also had a large personality, which he used to his advantage in and out of court.

Scholl knew his way around the courthouse and around the county. He had lived in Oneida County virtually his whole life and had practiced law there for nearly 20 years when he was appointed to Kelly's case. He couldn't walk into the courthouse without half a dozen people greeting him. Usually he would stop and chat a moment, share a joke. He also had a good relationship with the lawyers in the local district attorney's office and a proven track record for negotiating favorable pleas.

But Kelly was not interested in a plea; she was determined to go to trial. So that's what Scholl prepared to do. The only problem was that Scholl had never tried a murder case. He wasn't happy that his first murder trial would be on behalf of a young woman with no record who insisted she was innocent.

It's not that Scholl had no trial experience at all. He had tried a handful of cases, but nothing approaching a murder trial. When a violent felony was committed in the county, the local public defender usually handled it. But the public defender was representing Billy Ronald, and it would have been a conflict of interest for him to represent Kelly as well. Ethical rules prohibit a lawyer or law firm from representing people who might point the finger at each other.

When Scholl first saw Kelly at the local jail, he couldn't help but think of his own daughter. Though Kelly was a few years older, she still looked like a teenager. Like his daughter, Kelly knew nothing about the workings of criminal law. She didn't understand how she had come to be indicted, extradited, and held without bail hundreds of miles from her family. She had nobody but Scholl looking out for her. What if his daughter had gone for a drive with a guy who turned out to be a killer? What if she was in a jail cell far from home? *There but for the grace of God,* he thought.

Scholl dedicated himself to Kelly's case. Before trial, he went to the prosecutor and told him there was a real possibility they had the wrong person and the actual accomplice was still out there. He pointed to the shaky eyewitness identification, the lack of corroboration, the problem of guilt by association. The prosecutor was unmoved. Scholl asked the prosecutor to at least agree to separate trials. Billy Ronald had acknowledged that he had the car and Kelly was not with him at the time of the crime. He would say so if Kelly was tried separately but would "take the Fifth" at a joint trial. The prosecutor was unmoved.

It was a shocking crime: A teenager had been butchered for a couple hundred dollars. Hatch had just graduated from high school, where he had been a star athlete. He was to begin college in the fall. He left behind grieving parents, a twin brother, and many friends.

"This is a big case for a small town," the prosecutor told Scholl. Sherrill had never had such a brutal killing. The town of Sherrill, where the crime occurred, is known as the smallest "city" in New York. Calling it a city is a stretch. If you blink while driving through, you could miss Sherrill entirely; it is only two square miles with a current population of just over 3,000.

The prosecutor believed in the police investigation, and the police believed that Kelly was involved. The best he could do was offer a plea to robbery, which carried a sentence of 5 to 15 years in prison. "Maybe your client only meant to rob the place and didn't know what her boyfriend was up to," the prosecutor said to Scholl. "If that's true, she would be wise to take the deal."

Onerous though it may be, many lawyers find it hard to resist an innocent client. John Adams said: "It is of more importance to [the] community that innocence should be protected than it is that guilt should be punished, for guilt and crimes are so frequent in the world. . . . But when innocence itself is brought to the bar and condemned . . . there [is] an end to all security whatsoever."[18]

A lawyer who seeks the vindication of a wrongly accused person turns to the law for truth and justice, concepts that don't always come together in our system. It is consistent with our adversary system of criminal justice that guilty people sometimes get off. We can live with this because, to paraphrase the maxim attributed to English jurist Sir William Blackstone, it is better that ten guilty people go free than one innocent person suffer.

Though lawyers serve the system by diligently representing both the guilty and the innocent, a lawyer who represents an innocent client can't help but feel that she is doing more.

Representing the innocent is also the best, the ultimate, the irrefutable answer to the Question. The criminal lawyer declares with confidence: "How can I represent those people? Because some of them are *innocent*." The person who posed the Question is rendered mute. Suddenly he or she is looking at the lawyer with something approaching respect. These are the people lawyers *should* represent. There is no need for explanation or apology. Conversation over.

It is not surprising that Innocence Projects, which seek to exonerate factually innocent prisoners through DNA evidence, have sprung up at law schools all over the world. Students previously uninterested in criminal defense now flock to represent the innocent. These students have grown up in a culture with overwhelmingly positive images of law enforcement. Television shows like *Law and Order, CSI,* and their endless spin-offs seem to be on the air 24 hours a day. Yet even *Law and Order* star Sam Waterston, the personification of prosecutorial rectitude, would approve of defending the innocent.

Many lawyers go into criminal defense with the image of the wrongly accused in mind. I often tell students that I became a criminal lawyer because I read *To Kill a Mockingbird* too many times as an impressionable child. The story of Tom Robinson, an honest black man falsely accused of rape by a troubled white woman, grieved and ultimately inspired me. I wanted to be like Atticus Finch, the lawyer who championed Robinson's cause. Could there be nobler work?

Yet clients who maintain their innocence can be complicated. Many clients say they are innocent. They do so for a variety of reasons. They think a lawyer will work harder for them if the lawyer believes they're innocent. Experienced lawyers expect clients to protest their innocence, especially when the charge is serious. No one likes to go gentle into the night.

There is also a risk for lawyers who trumpet their innocent clients. Lawyers who declare publicly—to a colleague, a prosecutor, a judge—that they have an innocent client run the risk of being considered gullible, naive, suckers. These are lawyers who have lost their professional judgment and have been taken in by a manipulative client. And they don't even know it.

Kelly rejected the robbery plea. She told Scholl that she didn't rob anyone, she had nothing to do with what happened at the Seaway station, and she couldn't plead guilty to a crime she didn't commit. Scholl urged her to give the offer serious thought. He explained that there were no guarantees at trial and Kelly was facing a life sentence. If the eyewitness positively identified her as being at the scene of the crime, she could very well be found guilty. Kelly would likely be tried together with Billy Ronald, Scholl said, and since the evidence against him was so damning, and the crime so brutal, it could well spill over to Kelly.

But Kelly could not consider taking the plea. She could not begin to weigh the plea offer—the 5 to 15—against her chances of being found guilty and being sentenced to life in prison. She couldn't do this because she was innocent. She could not imagine that a jury would ever find her guilty when she *wasn't.* It was as simple as that.

Scholl tried to point out that, between the extradition process in North Carolina and her pretrial detention in New York, Kelly had already been locked up for nearly a year. With good behavior, she could be out in three and a half years. She would still be young enough to put this ordeal behind her and resume her life.

Kelly wouldn't hear of it. Taking the plea—standing in a courtroom and saying that she had committed a crime she had not committed—was unthinkable. It was out of the question. It didn't even make sense. Kelly was not a criminal. How could she say that she was? She had never robbed or killed anyone; she had never committed *any* crime. Kelly had never been in a situation like this before. Prior to her arrest, she had never even been in court. She had never talked to a lawyer. The whole situation—having a lawyer, the lawyer advising her to take a plea, the lawyer talking about the possibility of life in prison—was completely foreign to her.

Kelly also had a patriotic view of the legal system: She believed in the American system of justice. She believed in judges and juries. She was sure that if she told the truth, she would be believed and everything would be okay. Although the system had failed her so far—it had allowed her to be arrested, taken away from home, and jailed—it would come through for her in the end.

But it didn't.

Although Scholl did his best, immersing himself in the trial, trying hard to attack the state's case, giving an impassioned closing argument that went on for nearly an hour, the jury came back with a guilty verdict. Scholl was nearly as anguished by the verdict as Kelly was. Toward the end of the trial he had begun to believe that she had a chance. He even brought his 14-year-old son to court one day, something he would not have done if he thought things were going badly.

When the jury was dismissed, Scholl asked the trial judge to set aside the verdict because the evidence was insufficient to support a conviction. He called the verdict a serious miscarriage of justice. He said an innocent person had been convicted. The judge denied Scholl's motion.

After Kelly was convicted, she was sent to one prison and then another. With the help of a jailhouse lawyer—Kelly didn't know how to go about getting a real appellate lawyer—she appealed her conviction in state appeals court. The appeal was denied. With help from the same inmate, she appealed to New York's highest court. That appeal was denied.

Time passed.

❦

I was thrilled when I got into the New York University Prison Law Clinic as a second-year student. Third-year students had priority, and second-year students were accepted only after every interested third-year student got in. Amazingly, I managed to persuade the director of the clinic, Claudia Angelos, to choose me for one of the few remaining slots.

I wanted to work with prisoners—I went to law school to represent the poor, and prisons are the land of the poor—and I wanted to work with Claudia. I had seen her around the law school in her boots, short skirts, and dangling silver earrings. She was young, smart, and hip. She had gone to the best schools—Radcliffe College and Harvard Law School—but she had chosen a different path from most with her academic pedigree. Claudia had never been interested in a conventional legal career, especially a commercial one. She wasn't interested in working for the rich or connected; she wanted instead to work for the least powerful. She had been a prisoners' legal services lawyer before becoming a law teacher and was proud of it. Her office was full of thank-you notes from prisoners and their photographs (sometimes with a smiling Claudia). There were also pictures of prisoners' kids.

For as long as I can remember I felt drawn to the struggles of the poor and marginalized, including people who committed crimes. I also felt drawn to those who advocate for people at the margins. Their life's work would be mine, too, and I wanted to be part of their society. One astute commentator describes criminal defense lawyers as a "breed unto themselves" and lists these identifying characteristics:

1. They are mostly Italian, Jewish, or Irish males.
2. There are females, as well, but not many, and they, too, are mostly Italian, Jewish, or Irish.
3. The males are often quite short. Cheap sidewalk analysis indicates that, as children, they were forced to fight for their honor among bigger, stronger classmates, thus becoming "defensive."
4. Surprisingly, many of them will admit to a very upscale education, often Ivy League or something like William & Mary or Stanford.

5. They can't complete a sentence that doesn't include the F-word. The more frequently and creatively it's used, the more effectively they feel they've communicated (e.g., "I ordered a f__ing tuna salad on wheat, and that flea-brained f__ brought me a ham and cheese on pumper-f__ing-nickel").

6. They're often ill at ease with people who are not themselves criminal defense lawyers.

7. They cry in public if the subject has to do with justice or the death penalty.

Among their aberrations:

1. They dress outrageously, usually in blue jeans and t-shirts that say unprintable things. When they must dress for court, however, they have the best ties anywhere (men) or the most expensive dresses and jewelry (women).

2. They wear their hair too long (men) or skirts too short (women).

3. They never plan ahead. Ever.

4. They abuse substances and are sexually promiscuous well into their 30s. After that they mellow somewhat, but the profanity never goes away.

5. Oddly, they make loving parents.[19]

As a not terribly tall Jewish woman, with an "upscale education" (Yale College and NYU Law School), a tendency toward profanity (some words are just more *expressive* than others, especially the adjective form of the f-word), a secret (well, maybe not so secret) preference for the company of other criminal defense lawyers, a lifelong abhorrence of the death penalty, a lifelong love for shopping (especially for clothes and jewelry, even though I am basically a well-worn Levi's and T-shirt type), a decent pair of legs (hence the short skirts of my youth), an aversion to planning (why can't things just happen when they happen, what is wrong with spontaneity?), and a son on whom the sun rises and sets, it is uncanny how well I fit the aforementioned defender prototype.

There is no easy explanation for why I felt drawn to indigent criminal defense, which I have come to regard as a calling. No doubt my interest in indigent criminal defense had something to do with an early political and race consciousness. I attribute my politics (which started out liberal and moved steadily left through college and law school) to my mother, a lifelong liberal Democrat who always had a natural empathy for the needy and disadvantaged. My sensitivity to race is a product of the times in which I grew up and the influence of one particular African American woman who was and remains a force in my life. Sometimes I think I do what I do for my clients' mothers, most of whom are African American women.

On the first day of class in the prison law clinic, Claudia presented the case docket. Students were supposed to choose the cases they wanted to work on based on her description. Most of the cases involved prisoners at Sing Sing or Bedford Hills with civil legal problems. Some prisoners had family problems, a divorce or a child custody dispute. Some had health problems. Others had problems relating to government benefits. The cases all sounded interesting, and Claudia had nice things to say about every client. Then she talked about an unusual case the clinic had taken on, a post-conviction challenge. The clinic didn't ordinarily get involved in such work, but the superintendent of Bedford Hills Prison had called Claudia personally and asked her to take the case of a young woman named Patsy Kelly Jarrett. Jarrett was from a small town in North Carolina, had no prior record, and had been convicted of a murder and robbery she maintained she did not commit. The superintendent had looked into the case and believed that Jarrett may have been wrongfully convicted. Jarrett had no money to hire a lawyer to pursue an appeal in federal court. She needed Claudia and her students.

I raised my hand immediately to work on Jarrett's case. No other case compared. This was why I had come to law school.

I also took on other cases. I was eager for experience, and it was exciting to be working for real people in need instead of sitting in class. It was surprising and reassuring how readily our clients accepted us as lawyers. No matter how young and inexperienced we were or how sophisticated and experienced they were, the prisoners seemed happy for our help.

One of my first clients aside from Kelly was a brilliant jailhouse lawyer imprisoned at Sing Sing. He had what sounded to me like a routine civil legal problem. He came down to our first interview sporting lawyerly looking steel-rimmed glasses and carrying a thick accordion folder full of legal papers. I felt like an imposter. He should have been *my* lawyer.

Another client at Bedford Hills had sought assistance from the clinic because she had a lump on her breast, and the prison was failing to provide adequate treatment. She had repeatedly asked to go to the local hospital for an X-ray, but the prison infirmary kept telling her to monitor the lump's growth. During my first meeting with this client, she introduced herself and then immediately got down to business. She opened her blouse and revealed a lump the size of a golf ball. She said to me, "Feel this." In desperate need of supervision—was feeling a client's breast consistent with good professional boundaries?—I looked around the room for Claudia, but she wasn't there. The client was waiting, blouse unbuttoned. I tried to say, "Yes, I see"—figuring this acknowledgment would obviate the necessity of me actually touching the client's lump—but she wouldn't let me get away with anything less than physical contact. She took my hand and made me feel her breast. She was smart to do it. Although I had never seen or felt a cancerous tumor before, there was no question about what I was feeling. I drafted an emergency motion that day.

Under Claudia's guidance and direction, I worked on Kelly's petition for a writ of habeas corpus, through which prisoners challenge their convictions in federal court, for the next two years. I must have gone through her trial transcript 100 times, reading and rereading it, indexing it, scrutinizing the testimony of witnesses, incorporating useful bits into the petition. I became an expert on identification law. I became an expert on the law of "severance" (to the extent there is any law—mostly, there is enormous judicial discretion about whether defendants accused of taking part in the same offense may be tried together). Under Claudia's tutelage, I learned to be both creative and careful in arguing the law.

As part of my work on the case, another clinic student and I took a trip down to State Farm, Virginia, to pay a visit to Billy Ronald in prison. He was serving his Danville murder sentence first at a dreary-looking maximum-security facility called the Powhatan Correctional Center and would serve the Sherrill murder sentence in New York only after he served his Virginia time. The plan was to meet with Billy Ronald and get him to sign an affidavit exonerating Kelly. Even though we knew that the word of a twice-convicted murderer would not carry much weight, we figured it couldn't hurt. We also wanted to have something in writing from Billy Ronald—something along the lines of what he had conveyed to Scholl during the severance proceedings, and maybe a more explicit statement about what exactly happened on August 11, 1973. We prepared a number of possible affidavits for his signature.

It was fascinating to meet Billy Ronald face to face. I knew very little about him then, and the image in my mind was much more sinister than the man I encountered. He was polite if a bit guarded. He had a slight build, much smaller than I had pictured, and was nice looking—clean shaven, kind of a pretty face, piercing eyes, dark head of hair. When we told him about Kelly, he listened but didn't ask any questions. He was unwilling to sign an affidavit admitting that he committed the crime, because he wanted to preserve his right to appeal. But he was willing to say that he had Kelly's car for the 24-hour period that included the time of the crime, that Kelly was not with him during that time period, that he often had use of Kelly's car on his own, and that Kelly did not know his whereabouts or actions when he had use of her car. He was unwilling to identify who was with him in the car on August 11 and refused to discuss the person we believed was with him: a man named William Sullivan, whom Billy Ronald had dated that summer. He said that was the best he could do for us. We took the signed affidavit and thanked him for his time.

I visited Kelly at the prison on a monthly basis, sometimes more. I wanted to keep her informed of what we were doing on her case, to know which issues we were exploring and raising. I wanted to keep her company.

I fretted about her. The more I got to know her, the more bizarre and frightening her incarceration seemed to me. I thought about how mind-boggling it must be for her: One minute she was a North Carolina farm girl and the next, a New York prisoner. One day she was wearing jeans and a sleeveless gingham shirt tied at the waist, and the next she was in dark green dungarees and work shirt, a number stitched above her left breast. It was remarkable that she was still standing. I felt fairly certain that I wouldn't have been.

Armed with a little knowledge of psychology, I figured Kelly must still be suffering from the trauma of having been arrested, prosecuted, and convicted for something she didn't do. Probably the trauma would never lift.

I was haunted by the idea of being locked up because of a mistaken identification. I had never really thought about such a thing happening—except in the most abstract way, or when a movie like Alfred Hitchcock's *The Wrong Man* was broadcast on late-night TV—until Kelly. But now I felt horrified by how often eyewitnesses probably made mistakes, by the randomness of it. It could happen to anyone.

I used to walk around New York's Greenwich Village, where I lived during law school, thinking about Kelly and wondering what it must have been like to be plucked from her home and jailed for something she had nothing to do with. I wondered what it must have been like to go on a six-week road trip with someone who turned out to be a psychopath and to pay for it for the rest of your life. I wondered how Kelly made sense of it all, knowing that, of course, she couldn't because it made no sense. I wondered whether she would ever make peace with it—if anyone could.

I felt guilty sometimes, that I was me and she was Kelly, and I had the freedom to walk around the West Village fretting about her.

There were a couple of record stores I used to haunt during law school. I always thought of Kelly when I was shopping for records. I would say to myself, *Here I am shopping for records. How can I be doing such a frivolous thing when Kelly is locked up?*

I confess that I bought the records anyway.

The process of writing and filing the petition was painstaking and slow. This was partly because of the nature of the project: It was difficult to formulate an effective federal constitutional challenge to Kelly's conviction when the mistakes at trial were mostly factual (the witness made a mistake), not legal (as when the judge makes a mistake). To get into federal court, we needed plain legal error—the trial judge erred in allowing unreliable identification testimony in evidence, for example. The sluggish pace also had to do with Kelly being represented by a law school clinic. The dual function of a clinic to represent clients and to educate students means that things take longer.

I had my own experience as a consumer of services provided by a university clinic—the NYU Dental School. For a money-strapped law student in need of a dentist, the least expensive alternative was the clinic. The care I received was excellent, but I had to keep my mouth open for hours.

The habeas petition was filed after I graduated from law school and had joined the public defender's office in Philadelphia. I was glad to receive a copy, but I was engrossed in my new life and new career. I was a lawyer now, a public defender. My hands were full. I kept in touch with Kelly, but our contact was sporadic. I thought about her sometimes—when I had a case with an identification issue, when I'd come upon a newspaper story about the release of a wrongly convicted prisoner, during softball season (we were both infielders).

I had been a defender for three years when Claudia called to tell me that Kelly's habeas petition had been granted by the federal district court in Manhattan. I was overjoyed. This was an amazing, against-the-odds victory. I couldn't believe that Kelly had prevailed after all this time, that justice had prevailed. The court had accepted all of our arguments about the wrongful admission of identification evidence at trial. The court even expressed concern about an innocent person being unjustly convicted. Claudia was pleased with the ruling but worried about the future. The state will appeal, she said. And the federal appeals court will be a much tougher forum.

Claudia was right. The state appealed, and the case was scheduled for argument before the United States Court of Appeals for the Second Circuit. Before the case was heard, the state made an offer to Kelly: If she pled guilty, she would receive a sentence of time served. This meant that she would be released from prison and could go home. Kelly had served 10 years. She had already spent a decade of her life in a maximum-security prison. Kelly refused the plea offer. She told Claudia that she couldn't do it, couldn't plead guilty to a crime she did not commit. The crime was too horrible. She didn't think she would be able to live with herself if she admitted having taken part in a senseless, brutal murder of a teenager that she had had nothing to do with. She didn't think she would be able to look herself in the mirror. She didn't think she would be able to face anyone she knew.

Kelly also believed she would be vindicated by the court of appeals.

Six months after the district court granted Kelly's petition, the court of appeals reversed. It disagreed with the lower court's interpretation of the law of identification, held that the eyewitness testimony was properly admitted, and reinstated Kelly's conviction.

The question of how hard a lawyer should lean on a client to take a plea is a difficult one. The lawyer must balance respect for client autonomy against his or her professional obligation to counsel the client. While it is true that the client ultimately decides whether to plead guilty or go to trial—clearly, the most important decision in a criminal case—this does not mean that the lawyer should meekly defer to a client's inclination. Sometimes effective counseling—*getting through* to a client about the reality of his or her situation—means leaning very, very hard.

As prominent lawyer and legal scholar Anthony Amsterdam has written:

> [C]ounsel may and must give the client the benefit of counsel's professional advice on this crucial decision; and often counsel can protect the client from disaster only by using a considerable amount of persuasion to convince the client that a plea which the client instinctively disfavors is, in fact, in his or her best interest. This persuasion is most often needed to convince the client that s/he should plead guilty in a case in which a not guilty plea would be destructive. The limits of allowable persuasion are fixed by the lawyer's conscience.[20]

Claudia does not think this question is difficult or complex. She believes it was her responsibility to persuade Kelly to take the plea in 1986, and she blames herself for not pressing Kelly hard enough. She blames herself for the 19 years that Kelly served after she rejected the plea offer. Although Claudia advised Kelly to take the plea, told her that she was lucky to win in the district court, warned her that she would likely lose in the appeals court, and told her that if she were in Kelly's shoes she would take the plea, she believes she accepted Kelly's decision too readily. She failed to exert enough pressure.

There are many questions here. Should Claudia have "made" Kelly take the plea, telling her that she could seek vindication outside the prison walls? Was Claudia too deferential to her client's "autonomy" at the expense of her professional obligation to get

Kelly to do the wise thing? What was in Kelly's interest here—getting out of prison or having peace of mind, her freedom or her dignity? Would getting out under spurious circumstances—saying she did something that she did not do—have so damaged Kelly's sense of herself that the freedom she would have obtained would somehow be *less free?* Did Kelly mean it when she said that she wouldn't be able to live with herself if she pled guilty, or was she only trying to express how difficult it would be for her to do it? While in prison, Kelly had converted to Catholicism. What if she was basing her decision on misplaced faith—either in the system (she had, after all, won in the district court) or in God (she had become more and more devout as the years passed)? Did Kelly fully understand that this might be the one chance—the only chance—she had to avoid spending her entire life behind bars? Did she know that this was the moment for her, and everything else would be consequence?

Who was in a better position to know what was best for Kelly, Claudia or Kelly?

This last question is harder than it may seem. While Claudia holds herself responsible for Kelly's refusal to take the plea—she believes that because of their good, trusting relationship she could have gotten Kelly to accept it—Kelly disagrees. Claudia regards her failure to get Kelly to take the plea as the worst mistake of her professional career. Again, Kelly disagrees. Kelly insists that she was right to refuse the plea and that nothing Claudia could have said would have changed her mind. She says if she had it to do over again, she would again turn down the plea.

Kelly's continued insistence that it was *her* decision to refuse the plea and that she was right to do so does not comfort Claudia. She says she takes responsibility for "Kelly taking responsibility." She believes she set things in motion so that Kelly bore the burden of the decision alone, and this was wrong. Claudia says she would feel better if she had bullied Kelly into taking the plea, even if later Kelly resented her for it. At least Kelly would have been free.

For Claudia, the worst part is that at the time she conveyed the plea offer to Kelly, she was fully conscious of the gravity of the situation and had no doubt that Kelly should take the plea. She believes she bought in an overly academic notion of "client-centeredness" and lacked the criminal defense experience to temper it. She was a prisoners' rights lawyer representing civil plaintiffs. She did not have a veteran criminal lawyer's perspective about clients' hostile reactions to plea offers, especially in serious cases. She had never exercised a "considerable amount of persuasion" to induce a recalcitrant client to take a plea.

Experienced criminal defense lawyers know that there are many possible meanings to clients' initial refusal to take a plea, most of which also apply to their initial assertion of innocence. Clients might be expressing unhappiness at their situation, or anger at the system. Clients might be testing the lawyer, making sure he or she does everything possible on their behalf. Some clients might be telling the lawyer that they won't go down without a fight, that they'd rather be convicted at trial and sentenced to prison than go to the gallows willingly. Other clients might be masking a range of feelings from having committed an embarrassing, shameful, or hateful act; it is easier to deny the conduct than admit guilt and face family and friends. Clients might be expressing their assessment of the evidence in the case. Still others might simply be seeking a lawyer who *believes* in them in the broadest possible way.

It is impossible to know why Kelly insisted that she would never take a plea—that if she were still in prison today and someone said *I will let you out of here right now if you just say you're guilty,* she would say no. It could be a matter of principle or conscience. It could also be that she cannot bear to think that she rejected the one opportunity she had to free herself for no reason other than principle and was incarcerated for nearly 20 more years as a consequence. Principle seems small comfort after decades in prison.

While Kelly was imprisoned, she lost everything: her parents, her youth, her childbearing years, the life she once knew. Still, she claims she would never have taken a plea. When I tell her that I would have made her take such a plea if I had had the chance, she is quiet.

Kelly was now serving a life sentence with no legal remedy. Claudia had consulted some of the most prominent criminal appellate lawyers in the country and they confirmed this awful fact: Kelly's case could not be brought before the U.S. Supreme Court because there were no "cognizable" legal issues—no distinct and important questions of law for the Court to review—only factual ones. Kelly was wrongly convicted not because the judge made a mistake in his evidentiary rulings or instructions to the jury but because the lone eyewitness incorrectly identified Kelly, and the jury believed him. These were factual, not legal, errors, which cannot be appealed.

Although Claudia and her students had fashioned a legal argument for the federal habeas petition, it was a creative argument. Ordinarily, there needs to be a finding of "suggestiveness"—that the police did something to skew the identification process—

before the court considers whether an identification has an independent, reliable basis. Kelly's petition had argued that the eyewitness identification was so weak—in view of the witness's limited observation and scant description—that it could only be the product of police suggestion.

There was little in the record to support a claim of suggestion. The best argument was that the police-compiled photo spread contained only females when the eyewitness had equivocated about the driver's gender. Although Kelly's photograph was marked "sheriff department," another photograph also had a law enforcement stamp. Otherwise the photos consisted of women who were roughly the same age, race, coloring, and build. The argument on reliability was much stronger. Here was a witness who did not know the person he had seen, had seen the person for a matter of seconds, had no particular reason to pay attention, and had been unable to describe the person in any detail shortly after the observation.

Although the federal district court adopted the defense formulation in a strongly worded decision, the court of appeals rejected this approach. The law was clear, the higher court ruled, that evidence of police suggestion was required before the court addressed the question of reliability. It was for the jury to weigh the eyewitness's testimony and determine guilt or innocence.

The unfortunate reality is that, once convicted, victims of mistaken identification are all but doomed. Unless there is clear police or prosecutorial error, or the presence of someone else's DNA, the chances of prevailing on appeal are slim. Mistaken identification cases are always about factual, not legal, errors. Trial lawyers win mistaken ID cases, not appellate lawyers.

At trial, the eyewitness was certain that Kelly was the person he had seen in the car. When Kelly's lawyer pressed him on this—pointing out the man's prior uncertainty, his identification of someone else's photograph, his failure to identify Kelly at a previous court hearing—the witness became increasingly adamant. Although studies have shown that a witness's certainty has little to do with the accuracy of identification, most people don't know this. It was during Scholl's cross-examination that the witness was at his most resolute.

It could be said that Kelly's innocence—the fact of her innocence, her commitment to it—stood in the way of any chance for freedom. If she hadn't rejected the initial plea offer of 5 to 15, she could have been out as early as 1980, when she was only 29. Kelly served an additional 25 years not for the crime but for refusing to admit to it. If she hadn't rejected the plea offer generated by the favorable district court ruling, she could have been out as early as 1986, when she was only 35. She served another 19 years not for the crime but for refusing to admit to it.

Arguably, both plea offers reflected the state's view that Kelly's alleged conduct merited considerably less than life in prison had she only been willing to say she did it. But she was not.

It could also be said that Kelly's innocence got in the way of her judgment.

Kelly is not the first innocent person—nor is she unique among criminal defendants generally—to exercise shaky judgment when confronted with an important life decision. Innocent or guilty, it is difficult to exercise good judgment when facing a lengthy prison sentence. The most savvy and experienced defendant can become paralyzed when deciding between one long sentence and the possibility of an even longer one.

It might be hardest when the accused are innocent. Generally speaking, good judgment in the face of a plea offer requires an ability to objectively assess the evidence and weigh existing options while at the same time identifying personal values: family, community, work, faith, freedom, conscience. Then the accused must decide which of these values they are willing to risk or sacrifice and how much risk they can bear. To an innocent person, this entire discussion is an outrage. Though "innocence" could be regarded as one more thing to consider, it doesn't feel that way to those who actually are innocent. It feels like the only thing.

There are exceptions.

Some years after meeting Kelly, I had a client who was accused of felony child abuse. The specific allegation was that my client shook a baby so hard it caused cerebral hemorrhaging. The prosecution's case was circumstantial, since no one had actually seen my client shake or otherwise harm the baby. The chief prosecution witness was a neurologist who claimed to be able to pinpoint the time of the incident, which was when the baby was in my client's care. My client was a woman with no criminal record, who was taking college classes in the hope of becoming a primary school teacher. She occasionally babysat for the injured baby, along with the baby's six siblings and several cousins, in the housing project where she lived. She babysat at the behest of the baby's aunt, who paid my client a few dollars an hour to watch the kids so she could go out.

My client maintained that she was innocent and that the baby was fine when the aunt returned home. She believed that something must have happened after she left. Investigation backed her up. When defense investigators went to the aunt's house, it was in shambles, and life there was clearly chaotic. There were babies teetering unstrapped on high chairs, toddlers looking like they hadn't been bathed in weeks, and slightly older children who appeared to be suffering from brain injury themselves. The place reeked of a combination of dog urine, human feces, and stale cigarette smoke. The baby was living with her aunt because her mother, a crack addict, was undergoing drug rehabilitation. The aunt had a documented history of involvement with the child welfare authorities for neglect and abuse.

I believed my client was innocent and went to the prosecutor—but reluctantly, because prosecutors are seldom receptive to claims of innocence and there are significant risks. Too often, defense lawyers share information that would be better saved for trial and get little in return. But I felt strongly that this prosecution should not go forward and decided, on balance, that it was worth a try. I shared what we had uncovered through investigation and urged the prosecutor to talk to the aunt. I also urged him to talk to the children who were present that day, including my client's own two (well-cared-for) children. I said I would consider allowing him to talk to my client.

To my surprise, the prosecutor took what I said seriously and agreed to conduct further investigation. Perhaps he already had his own misgivings. After looking into the case, he agreed there were problems. As a result, he was willing to make my client an offer: In exchange for a guilty plea, he would reduce the felony child abuse charge to a misdemeanor. Instead of facing a 5-year mandatory minimum sentence and the possibility of 20, my client would receive probation.

My client wanted to think about it. Even though she had done nothing wrong, she was terrified of being sent to prison and having her children placed in foster care. She had been willing to go to trial when the plea offer had been a 5-year prison sentence, but now there was a way to guarantee her freedom. Even though pleading guilty would be a lie—and there would be significant collateral consequences, including having a criminal record and never being able to work with children again—she was willing to live with this. Her children were the most important thing.

I was furious. Not at my client, but at the prosecutor. If he truly believed that my client had viciously assaulted a baby, causing severe and permanent brain damage, then he ought to pursue a felony conviction. If she had not done so—if someone else was the likely culprit—then the charges should be dismissed. Offering probation under these circumstances was the worst kind of prosecutorial coercion. My client might very well take the deal not because she was guilty but because she could not risk going to jail.

When I could not move the trial prosecutor, who believed he was being generous, I went to his boss, the chief of the child abuse unit. Softening my fury, I praised the trial prosecutor for taking another look at the case but argued that the current plea offer reflected serious doubts about it. I pointed out the coercive effect of an offer of probation on a mother of two young children and said it put me in the position of having to pressure my client go to trial rather than let her plead guilty to something she didn't do even though she was facing mandatory prison time if we lost. I said I shouldn't have to do that. I said I wasn't afraid of going to trial—which was partly true, because I believed we had a strong defense, but not entirely true because of course I was frightened because *my client was innocent*—but there should be no trial. I begged the child abuse chief to think hard about the wisdom of this prosecution.

In the end, this honorable prosecutor did what I asked. She thought hard about the case and dismissed it. I couldn't have been more grateful.

But it shouldn't have been necessary to go to a supervisor. It shouldn't have required "honor." The wise course—indeed, the ethical course—for any prosecutor under these circumstances would have been to decline to prosecute in the first place. Where there is a serious question about guilt, prosecutors are supposed to exercise their discretionary authority, not cede it to the jury. The paramount ethical obligation of prosecutors is to seek justice, not convictions. Any conscientious prosecutor would be wary of a serious, inflammatory charge supported more by innuendo than evidence.[21]

Kelly's prosecutor should have been mindful of the potential for injustice in a murder case resting on the testimony of a single, shaky eyewitness. In the years since Kelly's case, many prosecution offices have instituted special policies about one-witness identification cases. In Brooklyn, for example, a rule now requires the chief prosecutor to personally approve all felony cases involving one-witness identifications.[22] The Nassau County District Attorney's Office in New York has a "One Witness Committee" that regularly evaluates cases that rely on single-eyewitness testimony.[23]

In another case not long after the shaken baby case, I represented a man who admitted having committed a felony child sexual assault. Pumped up on drugs, he broke into a neighbor's home in the middle of the night and forced a prepubescent girl to perform oral sex on him. The client, a government employee with no prior record, had never done anything like this before and was deeply ashamed. He wanted to take responsibility for his wrongdoing by pleading guilty and thereby spare the victim further anguish.

I admired my client's candor and told him so. However, I also told him that a guilty plea was not in his legal interests. The only plea the government was offering would result in a mandatory minimum five-year prison sentence, a lot of time in view of his lack of prior record, history of employment, drug-impaired state at the time of the incident, and the number of witnesses who could testify about his otherwise good character. It was doubtful he would get more than five years if convicted at trial. I also believed we had a reasonable chance of winning at trial. The only evidence against the client was the girl's testimony, and at first she had told the police that she thought the intruder was her mother's boyfriend, which was enough to put forward the so-called SODDI defense (Some Other Dude Did It). I urged the client to look beyond his guilt and shame, and consider instead the fact that he had a wife and children, a loving home, a good job. He would lose everything if he pled guilty and went to prison as the lowest of the low: a child molester.

It took some time to convince this client to go to trial. He was surprised that his lawyer was advising against a plea when he was guilty and willing to say so. I said the decision was his, but it was my job to counsel him. What was his chief concern, aside from his conscience? I wondered. If he wanted to ensure that what he had done to the victim would never happen again, I told him it might make sense to undergo treatment. I said I would be glad to assist him in obtaining both drug and sex offender treatment, treatment he was unlikely to get in prison. After consulting with his wife, he decided to go to trial, where he was acquitted.

This is precisely the sort of story that makes people wonder about the morals of criminal lawyers and prompts the inexorable cocktail party Question. I did exactly what people fear most: I talked a guilty client—a child abuser, no less—into going to trial and got him off. I share this story not to expiate any wrongdoing on my part; I acted well within the bounds of professional ethics (though I acknowledge that the case posed some *personal* challenges for me, especially cross-examining the young girl). I share the story because it shows how difficult it is for clients—guilty or innocent—to make clear-headed judgments about their cases and their lives.

It's important to recognize that, like most defenders, I spend much more time persuading demonstrably guilty clients to plead guilty than avowedly guilty clients not to. These counseling sessions can be excruciating. In one case I spent hours—and too many jail visits to count—trying to convince a teenager charged with several violent felonies (including kidnapping, carjacking, and sexual assault) to cut his losses and take a plea. The case against him was overwhelming and included every possible kind of evidence: DNA, fingerprint, eyewitness identification, co-defendant testimony, and his own self-incriminating statements. If convicted at trial, which he surely would be, he would not get out of prison until he was a very old man. I managed to negotiate a plea that would have resulted in his release before he turned 40. The reduced plea reflected the client's youth and the fact that he had been high on PCP at the time of the crimes. But the client would have none of it. He regarded the plea deal as the same as a life sentence: Not only was 40 *old*, but he would never live that long in prison. I did everything I could think of to convince him otherwise—brought pictures of attractive celebrities in their late 30s, pointed out that he would be young enough at his release to start a family, and tried to talk through his understandable fear—but he wouldn't budge. He insisted on going to trial, where he was found guilty of all charges. He'll be lucky if he ever gets out of prison.

The point of these stories is that clients often act out of heated emotion, not cool reflection. They lack the perspective that a good lawyer is supposed to supply.

Kelly could not see beyond her innocence. Nothing else mattered. Consequently, she did not identify and weigh the things she cared about most: seeing her father before he died, helping her brother through his own hard times, making a difference outside the prison walls. Maybe her desire for vindication would have paled in comparison to the other things—and might have even seemed *selfish* in Kelly's own value system—if she had only lingered over the other issues a bit more. Claudia remains convinced that Kelly never distinguished between the fact of her innocence and the likelihood that a court would rule in her favor. She believes that Kelly's naiveté played a significant role in her rejection of the 1986 plea.

What's worse is Kelly did not see that she was choosing another value, namely *truth,* over everything else. She would not lie and say she was guilty even if she had to sacrifice both freedom and family.

Kelly was blinded by her faith as well. She was a religious woman. She would not put her hand on the Bible and swear to something that wasn't so; doing so would be taking God's name in vain. To lie would be to offend God in a literal sense, but worse, it would show a lack of faith in God. She would place her life in God's hands, through the hands of the jury. God would not forsake her.

Maybe, too, Kelly worried that her friends, family, and lawyers would not continue to believe in her if she took a plea.

Lawyers are supposed to maintain a level of distance from clients that allows for good, thoughtful advice built on experience and judgment. Still, the reality of an innocent client can affect a lawyer's judgment. When a lawyer believes that a client may be factually innocent—not merely that the prosecution or police have overcharged or overstepped, but they have the wrong person—it is harder to maintain appropriate distance. There is a heightened sense of responsibility when a lawyer undertakes the defense of an innocent person: Now the lawyer has both a professional and a moral responsibility to save the client. A terrible injustice will occur if the lawyer fails. The case inevitably becomes a cause.

Maintaining appropriate professional boundaries is not easy whether the client is guilty or innocent. Guilty clients can be as compelling as innocent ones. They are just as likable, or unlikable, as innocent clients. Most defenders would agree that the nature of the crime and the guilt or innocence of a client often has little bearing on the lawyer-client relationship. Lawyers are drawn to clients for the same reasons they are drawn to anyone: Some people are more appealing than others; some people inspire more empathy than others; sometimes it's a matter of chemistry. But with a guilty client, the lawyer can at least privately acknowledge that the client *did the crime* and thus bears some responsibility. Even if the client had a troubled, difficult childhood, this happened long before the lawyer arrived on the scene. There is built-in distance. There is only so much a lawyer can do. But with an innocent client, the client *didn't* do it, he or she bears *no responsibility* for it, so the lawyer had better be able to do something about it or else what is the point of being a lawyer? If a criminal lawyer can't save an innocent person, he or she might want to consider a different profession.

Most good lawyers find it harder to advise an innocent client to plead guilty than a guilty client to do the same, or a guilty client to plead not guilty. It doesn't matter that the factors underlying the advice are basically the same: the strength of the state's evidence, the strength of the defense, the likely sentence if convicted at trial, the likely sentence upon a guilty plea, the abilities and sensibilities of the judge and prosecutor, the client's values, the client's wishes. It doesn't matter that it is perfectly lawful for an avowedly innocent person to plead guilty under the 1970 Supreme Court case of *North Carolina v. Alford*.[24] There is something disturbing and distasteful about criminal lawyers urging innocent clients to plead guilty. It is the worst image of the court-appointed lawyer who works for the court and not the client, pushing one client after another into a plea. This is poor people's justice, assembly-line justice, no justice at all. Of course, even zealous, client-centered lawyers will admit that they occasionally urge innocent clients to plead guilty, but no one is happy about it. It feels bad to persuade an innocent person to plead guilty, even for good reasons. It feels cynical and corrupt.

But these feelings can get in the way of lawyerly judgment. Sometimes it is appropriate to advise an innocent client to plead guilty.

Going to trial on behalf of an innocent person is harder still. These are trials with endless days and sleepless nights. The lawyer cannot put in enough time before trial; there is never enough preparation. During the trial, no misstep or missed opportunity is insignificant. Every moment is critical. Every poorly phrased question or muddled argument can make or break the case. The lawyer must do much more than ably examine witnesses and make effective argument. The examinations must be masterful, the argument spellbinding, the entire performance nothing short of perfect.

◦～

Claudia believed Kelly was innocent, as had John Scholl before her. Although she had an activist's idealism, she was no easy touch. Kelly was not the first prisoner Claudia had met who claimed to be innocent. But Kelly's case was different. The one-witness identification coupled with the prospect of guilt by association put a chill in Claudia's heart. And Kelly herself was different. There was nothing grandiose or self-righteous about her assertion of innocence, or about having been the victim of a mistaken identification. Some clients are immersed in their own indignation. Kelly was at once steely and serene. She didn't need to put on a show; her innocence was self-evident.

Claudia may have been predisposed to believe in Kelly because of the extraordinary way the case had come to her. Prison superintendents rarely concern themselves with questions of guilt and innocence. These are matters decided by judges and juries. Superintendents do not usually trouble themselves with whether prisoners are well represented. Prison officials are often wary of lawyers. Claudia had never heard of a superintendent who was so disturbed by the possibility of an innocent prisoner that he sought out a defense lawyer to take the case. No one she knew had heard of such a thing.

It wasn't just the superintendent who felt this way about Kelly. Everyone Claudia met at Bedford Hills felt the same. Sister Antonia, a nun who ministered to Bedford Hills prisoners but who also believed in keeping a certain emotional separation from her charges, had become Kelly's godmother. She had no doubt that Kelly was a victim of mistaken identification, guilt by association, and inexperienced counsel. Sister Elaine, another prison chaplain, who was known for her work on the Children's Center, felt the same way. Kelly's social worker, her prison softball coach, the Catholic chaplain, the volunteers who came to the prison to conduct special programs all expressed the same concern about Kelly. Although most corrections officers pay little or no attention to prisoners' claims of innocence, nearly every one Claudia met said the same thing about Kelly: Something must be wrong with how her case went down because Kelly was no murderer, and if she had known what Billy Ronald had done she would have come forward.

Other prisoners felt the same way. A few years after Kelly was convicted, Jean Harris, the former headmistress of an exclusive private girls' school in Virginia, was sent to Bedford Hills following her conviction for the murder of her lover Herman Tarnower, the author of the best-selling book *The Scarsdale Diet*. Harris wrote about Kelly in a 1991 book, expressing a strong belief in her innocence:

> I spent this afternoon in the yard with a young woman I don't think I've ever mentioned to you. Her name is Kelly. I noticed her the first week I arrived. She had a freshness about her . . . a lovely, clear complexion, rosy cheeks, and a kind of complete innocence about her. She had come to Utica, New York, from a farm in High Point, North Carolina, looking for adventure, I suppose, fleeing from boredom, or perhaps fleeing from a small town's reaction to what was considered unforgivable there. Kelly is a lesbian.[25]

It is easy to dismiss this kind of talk as sentimental and subjective. Lawyers, corrections officers, prison volunteers, nuns, and other prisoners have no great wisdom about guilt and innocence. The evidence against an accused could be scant yet he or she could still be guilty. An eyewitness could have made his or her observations under poor circumstances and still be right about who did the crime. Murderers come in all different shapes and sizes. Murders happen in a variety of circumstances. The only thing that distinguishes a murderer from the rest of us is having killed.

It is also easy to dismiss even the most insistent, apparently earnest claim of innocence as opportunistic. An appealing, affable accused could swear up and down that she is innocent—and have everyone believing it—and be lying. People accused of crimes have been known to be less than completely truthful when they feel it is in their interest.

With Kelly, it wasn't her protestations of innocence that made people believe she was innocent. It was Kelly herself. It was what Jean Harris described as her "complete innocence." Even if Kelly had never been caught up in the criminal justice system, she would have been described as innocent. She was *an innocent*. She had an essentially trusting, guileless nature. It was this very personality trait that led her to believe that Billy Ronald was a safe traveling companion. Her trusting, unsuspecting nature led her to believe that a jury would see that she had committed no crime and acquit her. Later on, in prison, this same quality would lead her sometimes to confide in the wrong people.

Even after years of imprisonment, she was still untarnished. Though she had learned a hard truth about life, law, and justice, she still had an innocent heart. She believed in herself, in God, in goodness, in justice. She believed in people, even though many had failed her—first Billy Ronald, then her trial lawyer, the jury, the appellate courts. She was angry about what had happened to her—she railed against it sometimes, and cried about it when she was alone—but somehow she resisted bitterness. Her lawyers were more bitter than she was. It was as if she still couldn't believe that something as malicious as the Seaway crime could have happened, that someone she had been close to for a time had done it, and that she could have been caught up in it. It was still unfathomable to her. Something like this just isn't supposed to happen.

Some will doubt this grand innocence of Kelly's. They will offer a range of theories. Maybe she did something completely out of character and has convinced herself of her own innocence out of shock and distress. Maybe she was an unwitting accomplice to an awful crime and felt innocent. Maybe she was a witting accomplice to robbery but not murder. Maybe she could not reconcile the dissonance of being a good person but doing a bad thing and was in a state of psychological denial. Maybe, because she initially denied any knowledge of the crime—to the police, her family, her lawyers—she felt locked into that story and couldn't come clean. Maybe she simply could not face her friends and family and admit her involvement.

Maybe she honestly believes she didn't do it for whatever complicated set of reasons, though she in fact did it.

I understand the naysayers. It is difficult for some people to believe that Kelly had absolutely nothing to do with a crime that her friend, roommate, and traveling companion committed, in all likelihood using her car. It is difficult to take the word of a convicted prisoner whose conviction has been repeatedly upheld in court.

But Kelly isn't just any convicted prisoner. She has not merely claimed she was innocent; she twice turned down the chance to cut her sentence or get out altogether. As anyone who has spent any time in the criminal justice system knows, no guilty person would refuse a plea for release. Most would have grabbed the pre-trial robbery plea. No guilty person who had already served 10 years would have turned down an offer of time served, no matter how much faith that person had in God or the Court of Appeals for the Second Circuit. Guilty people benefit from plea bargaining. Innocent people do not.

Jean Harris wrote about this as well:

> Kelly was offered the opportunity to plea-bargain and have her sentence reduced. . . . Against the urging of most of her proba-bly wiser friends in prison, she refused to take the plea. "I didn't commit a crime. I never have nor would I rob a person or kill them, and I don't want to go through the rest of my life as a con-victed felon." She would be out of prison by now if she had taken the plea. I don't believe any guilty person after . . . years of incar-ceration would have turned down that plea.[26]

But a lawyer can also do a disservice to a client by signing on too quickly to a claim of innocence. The more the lawyer believes and cares about the client's innocence, the more locked in the client is. The client needs the lawyer and doesn't want to do anything to lose the lawyer's devotion. Soon the client stops sharing information or significantly edits what is shared. It becomes too risky for a guilty client to come clean with his or her lawyer: Suddenly the client is not only guilty but is a liar, manipulator, and betrayer.

Also, the lawyer who too readily believes a client can be per-ceived as gullible and naive by that client as well as by everyone else. The last thing a client wants is a fool for a lawyer. If the client can pull the wool over the lawyer's eyes, so will the prosecution. If the lawyer can't effectively take on a client, he or she is unlikely to effectively challenge the prosecution's witnesses. Most clients would swap a lawyer who believes them for one who will successfully fight for them.

Chapter 2

Truth

*L*ooking back, Utica, New York, was an unlikely place for a summer vacation. It was hardly a tourist destination then or now. Kelly didn't know anything about the city when she headed there in 1973. She knew that Billy Ronald had some friends there. But in her mind she was headed to *New York*—an exciting destination for a small-town girl who had only made it as far north as Washington, D.C. Upstate or down, it made no difference to Kelly. All she knew was she was going to the Empire State, the home of the Big Apple and the New York Yankees.

Located in the Mohawk River Valley, just southwest of the Adirondack Mountains, Utica is almost smack in the middle of the state. The nearest cities are Syracuse to the west (a one-hour drive), Binghamton to the south (two hours), Ithaca to the southwest (two hours), and Albany to the east (an hour and a half). Rochester is 140 miles due west, and Buffalo an additional 70. It takes at least four hours to drive to Utica from New York City.

Settled in 1773 on the site of Old Fort Schuyler, Utica was destroyed during the American Revolution and resettled afterward. The region's growth in the early part of the nineteenth century was sparked by its location on the Erie Canal, the middle section of which opened in 1820 and ran from Utica to Salina. The area developed further as other canals and railroads were built. At one time Utica had one of the largest freight yards on the New York Central railway system. From the late 1800s until the latter part of the 1900s, Utica was a bustling manufacturing center, drawing large numbers of immigrants and native-born Americans to the area. Among the goods manufactured were crushed stone and stone products, transportation equipment, tools and machinery, paper and leather goods, and textiles.

Starting in the late 1960s, manufacturing in the area began to decline and so did Utica's population. Over the past 40 years, the city has shrunk from 100,000 to less than 60,000. Utica is not especially pretty. Like the similar-size upstate towns of Schenectady and Troy, the physical surroundings are more appealing than the city itself. Just outside Utica you can go hiking in the foothills of the Adirondacks, bike through lush farmland, swim the area's lakes and ponds, or take a drive in the countryside.

Kelly enjoyed her time in Utica but seldom ventured outside the city. When she wasn't attending a softball game, she was spending time at Gerri's house or at the Hub. Once or twice she and Gerri caught a movie at the old Stanley Theater. They might have seen Ryan and Tatum O'Neal in *Paper Moon,* Barbra Streisand and Robert Redford in *The Way We Were,* or maybe *American Graffiti* with its ensemble cast—popular movies that summer.

Kelly liked the city's parks, especially those with well-kept softball fields. After a game, she would sometimes join Gerri's team for a picnic. Friends from the team kept inviting her to take a drive to one of the nearby lakes, but Kelly didn't want to go without Gerri. Gerri had late hours at the Hub, especially on weekends, and she and Kelly liked to sleep in and then putter around the house until it was time for work.

The days in Utica blended together. Kelly always wished she could remember more. But she didn't do anything special with her time except spend it with Gerri. They made an attractive pair: Gerri with her short-cropped brown hair and athletic build, and Kelly with her light brown pigtails and smaller, more feminine shape.

Sometimes they listened to music. Kelly, who was named after Patsy Cline, kept trying to get Gerri into country music. Her favorites were Charley Pride, Ronnie Milsap, Mel Tillis, Tammy Wynette, and Loretta Lynn. Kelly was delighted to find country radio up north. She had thought she would have to do without.

It has always been hard for Kelly to recall exactly what she did during those weeks in Utica, what Billy Ronald was doing, and how much she saw of him. When she was first questioned by New York state police officers, two other summers had passed, and there wasn't much to tell about them either. North Carolina summers had their own special feel: longer, lazier days, muggy heat, playing ball at night, going out for a soft-serve at the local dairy, hanging out at the gay bar. Once or twice a summer Kelly would take a drive to Myrtle Beach.

If Kelly had been asked to recall exactly where she was at a particular day and time during those intervening summers, she wouldn't have done very well either.

Though Kelly could not say exactly what she did from day to day in Utica—not in the days before the crime occurred, not in the days after, and, unfortunately, not on that fateful date—she has always known where she was *not* on August 11, 1973: She was not at a Seaway filling station in Sherrill, New York, helping Billy Ronald rob and kill the attendant.

~

Most people believe that trials are about finding the truth. They think that witnesses, lawyers, judges, and juries are engaged in the pursuit of truth.

Some believe a criminal trial is like a good whodunit. There may be twists and turns, but in the end, the truth will come out and the culprit will be caught.

But the truth can be murky. You think you know it—some things in life are surely knowable—and then it turns out you don't know the first thing about what happened. Sometimes there is no objective reality at all, just bits and pieces of individual experience and perception. What "really happened" turns out to be a matter of opinion. This has nothing to do with people "lying." As anyone who has spent time in a courtroom knows, even if every single witness tells the truth, there is no guarantee the truth will emerge.

The best cinematic portrayal of the flimsiness of truth and the power of subjective impression is the 1950 film *Rashomon,* by the great Japanese filmmaker Akira Kurosawa. *Rashomon* recounts the story of a rape and murder as told in flashbacks by four witnesses. Each of the witnesses feels a degree of blame for what occurred, which is reflected in their divergent accounts. In the end, it is impossible to determine what really happened. Now regarded as a classic, *Rashomon* has become a byword for any situation where truth is difficult to discern.

Fortunately, *proof,* not truth, is the currency in our court system. If truth is changeable and subjective, then proof is tangible, or at least testable. No matter how much we may want to know the truth at trial, proof is what counts. This is not always easy for people to accept, even those schooled in the law.

In teaching students about the role of truth in criminal defense, and in order to foster a criminal defense perspective, I employ an exercise. I write four concepts on the board: "Truth," "Justice," "Fairness/Equality," and "Client Interest." I then distribute index cards and ask the students to rank the concepts in order of importance as they undertake the defense of the indigent accused. When they have finished, we discuss the answers.

Many students select the first three concepts. They find the pursuit of truth, justice, and fairness/equality much more appealing than the prosaic pursuit of a client's interest. Young, idealistic students tend to care about such grand concepts; many report that these were the things that motivated them to come to law school. However, upon discussion, they soon recognize that truth, justice, and equality are aspirations, and vague ones at that, while pursuing the client's interest is what lawyers do as a matter of professional ethics.

After some initial resistance—people often feel strongly about the righteousness of their own motivations and values—students come to understand what public defender Martin Erdmann explained more than 30 years ago:

> Criminal law to the defense lawyer does not mean equity or fairness or proper punishment or vengeance. It means getting everything he can for his client. . . . Justice is a luxury enjoyed by the district attorney. He alone is sworn "to see that justice is done." The defense lawyer . . . finds himself most often working for the guilty and for a judicial system based upon the sound

but paradoxical principle that the guilty must be freed to protect the innocent.[1]

The only other "right answer" in an exercise intended to provoke
discussion is that truth should come in dead last. Even though
truth can be important (good defense lawyers should do their best
to uncover it, it will surely be used against the client, and it might
produce some useful investigative leads), the adversary system is
concerned only with proof. Moreover, because criminal defense is
most often about the representation of the factually guilty, truth is
often directly at odds with the client's interest.

The students learn—if not after the exercise then usually
upon representing their first clients—that, for the criminal defense lawyer, the client comes first, truth is either unknowable or
of little concern, and the other lofty motivations will fall where
they may.

Another way students and young lawyers come to understand
the issue of truth in advocacy is by recognizing that there are two
different sets of factual information in every case: "facts of the
world" and "facts of the case." The first set consists of everything
that can be known about the alleged crime, the witnesses, and the
accused. The second set consists only of the likely evidence at trial.
Criminal defense lawyers concern themselves almost entirely with
the latter, the facts of the case. The facts of the world are important only as they relate to the facts of the case.

As defenders construct a theory of the case, they spend
much of their energy trying to put the truth out of their minds.
They need to do this in order to critically evaluate the prosecution's case. It can be disheartening to look at the charging documents and police reports with their damning accounts of the

accused's conduct. Lawyers are tempted to throw up their hands in despair. What is the point, they wonder, in doing anything other than going directly to sentencing? But they remember: These are simply the allegations, they don't have to be taken at face value, there are always ways to mount a challenge. The police report's "truth" is one version of events. At the very least, this version ought to be tested.

By and large, I find the defense lawyer's relationship to the truth liberating. I like being unfettered by what really happened (to the extent this is knowable). I like being free to craft my own story. I like putting the pieces together in a puzzle of my choice. Criminal defense is art, not science. Skilled defenders can make something of nothing and nothing of something. Although I have been known to tell wishful-thinking clients that I am a lawyer, not a magician, under the right circumstances, a good criminal lawyer can make a case disappear.

When students complain about clients who fail to appear at the office for their initial interview—and every other appointment—I say this is not necessarily a bad thing. I tell them they are now free to develop a theory of the case based on the evidence or lack of evidence, without interference from the client. I explain exactly what this freedom means. They do not have to deal with ethical questions relating to clients who say one thing but want to testify to another. They do not have to bother with the tactical question of which is better, the client's story or a story that can be pieced together from the evidence. I say to them, "How lucky can you get? Not only are you not bound by the government's case, you are not even bound by your own client's story." I tell them the bottom line: "Don't let the details get in the way."

Students don't always see it this way. They want the defense to be moored to something. They want some version of truth, even if they often don't believe it. Students tend to operate in extremes: Either they believe all their clients, or all their clients are liars. They don't like to feel that they are making things up out of whole cloth. They want to the emperor to be wearing a little *something* even if it's flimsy.

Students are also upset about clients who seem uninterested in their cases. I try to get them to see that some cases might have more urgency for them than their clients, and for good reason. We talk about how their clients' daily struggle to provide for themselves and their families might take precedence. We talk about what any of us might do in their place if we were poor, homeless, drug addicted, without child care, or trying to hang on to a job that didn't allow us to come and go as we pleased, and we had an appointment with a lawyer about a misdemeanor arrest. Most students are able to provide diligent, zealous representation no matter how indifferent the client.

In some cases, the theory of defense may be that the truth of what happened is an existential question, as mystifying as the meaning of life. Before the right jury one can wax philosophic, but usually it's best to be simple, if vague. Life is complicated. Memory is complicated. Motive is complicated. When you make these kinds of arguments often enough, you start to believe them. Truth is simply an illusion, one illusion among many. No one can ever know what really happened. What at first sounds trite becomes profound.

Maybe this sleight of hand is not an entirely good thing. Perhaps it foments cynicism both among and about lawyers. There must be a difference between truth and invention. But trial lawyers are advocates: They are supposed to spin the facts to benefit the client. Trial lawyers are also storytellers: They are supposed to use the facts to tell the best possible story. Invention, therefore, is inevitable. As any good storyteller knows, too much truth can kill a story.

Kelly's truth was especially complicated.

When it became clear that Kelly and Billy Ronald would be tried together, Kelly's lawyer had a dilemma. He knew that the prosecution would do everything possible to link his client with Billy Ronald. According to the prosecution, the two were a latter-day version of Depression-era outlaws Bonnie and Clyde. Scholl had to figure out how to explain Kelly's relationship to Billy Ronald—how to unlink the two—without casting Kelly in a strange or bad light.

Scholl understood from Kelly that she was not romantically linked with Billy Ronald. Kelly had been clear from the start that she and Billy Ronald had not been sexually involved in Utica or anywhere else—that they were both gay.

In view of what her friendship with Billy Ronald had wrought, it was hard for Kelly to acknowledge to Scholl that at one time she had liked Billy Ronald. But she had. He was funny and quirky, and they had a good time together. He had a handsome face and a small wiry build. She liked the way he wore his long dark hair in a bandana, hippie style. Although he was six years her senior, he pursued her friendship. She had been flattered by his attention.

But those feelings had long since passed.

Kelly explained to Scholl that when she and Billy Ronald arrived in Utica, they immediately made themselves part of the gay community and went their own separate ways. Their shared accommodation was a matter of cost and convenience. Even though Billy Ronald was working and she was not, she didn't think of him as supporting her. The deal was that she provided the transportation and he provided the lodging. So long as Billy Ronald paid the rent, she didn't need to work.

She explained that, soon after arriving, she took up with Gerri and Billy Ronald took up with a man named William Sullivan. Sullivan was an effeminate-looking man in his 20s with shoulder-length brown hair, features that matched the description the witness gave of the second person at the Seaway. Kelly said that it might have been Sullivan who was in the car with Billy Ronald that day. She didn't know for sure, but it made sense. Billy Ronald spent a lot of time with Sullivan in Kelly's car.

Scholl wrestled with all this. He was not obliged to divulge Kelly's sexual orientation. He needed to figure out whether such a revelation would help or hurt Kelly's case. He wasn't sure what the police and prosecution knew about Kelly or the true nature of Kelly's and Billy Ronald's relationship. The police reports included interviews with people who had spent time with the two during the summer of 1973, and they seemed to regard them as a couple. Several referred to Kelly and Billy Ronald as "the Kellys." Scholl figured the prosecution would portray Kelly as Billy Ronald's girlfriend, his moll. He doubted they would say she was anything other than heterosexual.

Although revealing his client's lesbianism would have rebutted the depiction of Kelly and Billy Ronald as a couple, Scholl worried about the consequences of such a disclosure. He worried that jurors might be hostile to Kelly if they knew she was a lesbian—they might regard her as hard or "mannish," and hence capable of committing a violent crime, or just not one of them. Oneida County in 1977 was a fairly conservative place. Because Kelly was likely to testify, it was important that jurors be able to connect with her. So Scholl advised Kelly to keep secret, or at least downplay, the fact that she was a lesbian. If asked, Kelly was to say that she had "dated" Billy Ronald, but it had not been a serious involvement.

Kelly followed her lawyer's advice. When questioned by Scholl, she agreed that she had dated Billy Ronald. On cross-examination, when it became clear that the prosecution wanted to portray Kelly as both Billy Ronald's girlfriend and as a woman who liked other women, she denied being a "practicing lesbian."

There have been many criticisms of the criminal defense lawyer's indifference to truth. The critics include legal scholars, judges, members of the media, and ordinary citizens. Some commentators complain that criminal lawyers not only ignore and suppress the truth, they subvert it. They complain about defense lawyers putting forward false theories, keeping truthful and relevant evidence out of the trial, and making honest witnesses appear to be liars. While most critics acknowledge that defense lawyers act out of professional role and not poor character, they do so grudgingly. They say the system is deeply flawed and the defense lawyer is the chief purveyor of the flawed system.

The critics are right when they say that the system itself is not terribly concerned with truth. Although fact-finding is one function of our adversary justice system, it is not the only function. The system has a greater concern for process than outcome. There is an institutional commitment to ensuring fairness even at the expense of truth.

Still, what most critics fail to grasp when they complain about devious and deceitful defense lawyers is that criminal lawyers have multiple roles. We have little use for truth in advocacy but enormous regard for it elsewhere. I sometimes think that criminal lawyers spend more time telling the truth, indeed insisting on the truth, than any other actors in the criminal justice system.

This is because criminal lawyers are counselors as well as advocates. Given the relatively small number of cases that go to trial—some 95 percent are resolved by guilty pleas—criminal lawyers spend the bulk of their time counseling and advising clients. By counseling and advising, I mean working with clients to help them figure out what they want to do—chiefly, whether to go to trial or take a plea. Not to put too fine a point on it, I also mean *telling them what to do.*

We counsel and advise in jails and prisons, law offices, the courthouse hall. (As Lenny Bruce once quipped, "The only justice in the halls of justice is the halls.") Sometimes we go to our clients' homes to counsel them, enlisting the help and support of family members. These sessions can be hard going, often more challenging than going to trial. The most difficult part is telling our clients the truth about their cases and about their lives. We do so even though the truth is often unpleasant and may not endear us to our clients. We struggle with the temptation to soften the blow and allow for more possibilities than truly exist, but we know that we owe our clients the whole truth.

I continue to learn this lesson again and again. After several years of law practice, I had the occasion to counsel a client who wanted to go to trial in two separate drug distribution cases instead of pleading guilty to one case and having the other dismissed. The cases were assigned to the same judge, a judge who was known as a harsh sentencer after trial but a lenient sentencer after a guilty plea. I knew from experience that this judge would give the client close to the maximum sentence (30 years) if he went to trial and lost but would probably give him no more than 3 years if he pled guilty. I was supervising a young lawyer on the case who was taken with the affable client and believed that the police had planted the drugs. It seemed to me that she had not fully advised the client of the perils of trial. Based on the evidence in both cases—I had seen the police officers testify credibly at a pretrial hearing, and there was other corroborating evidence—I counseled the client hard to take the plea. The young lawyer privately complained that I was being too heavy-handed.

In counseling the client, I explained that he needed to win both trials in order to do better than the plea. This was because a conviction after trial on either case would result in a lengthy prison sentence. When the client asked what his chances were of winning both, I responded with what I thought was clear, unambiguous negativity. I said he had next to no chance of winning both cases. I said it was extremely unlikely, and he would be foolish to count on it. He said, "Can't you put it in numbers, like a 1-in-10 chance, or 50–50?" I said, "Not really." He said, "Come on, try, I'd like to know what kind of shot I have at winning both." I relented, saying, "Okay, if I must—you have a shot in a million of winning both cases."

After sleeping on it, the client announced the next morning that he had decided to go to trial instead of pleading. When I asked why, he used my words: "You told me I had a shot," he said. I was aghast. "I said it was a shot in a *million*." He said (this was during the heyday of the Chicago Bulls), "Michael Jordan had his shot and I'll take mine."

The client went to trial and was convicted. He received a sentence of 27 years, upon which the prosecution dropped the other case. The client was remarkably gracious. He thanked us for our efforts at trial and acknowledged that he should have listened to me about the plea. Still, I believe I should have been more forceful in my truth telling. I have never again used the word "shot" in advising clients. I avoid numerical calculations altogether.

I believe in being candid with clients; some would say blunt. I am this way about good news and bad, but, of course, it's harder to be blunt when the news is bad. But clients depend on their lawyers' judgment and advice. When the client's story stinks and there's no viable defense, we say so. When there is no getting around the government's case, we say so. When the client is facing years and years in prison, we say so. If it is unlikely the client will ever get out of prison, we say that too.

I had a client who was accused of participating in a murder—the shooting of a young man in front of several witnesses, some of whom knew my client by name. The client was shocked to find himself in this position and protested his innocence. He had a record of petty offenses only, and saw himself as a ladies' man who sold a little marijuana on the side, mostly to keep himself supplied. On the day of the crime, he was walking to the store when a carload of cronies pulled up. They offered him a ride, and he said sure. After a few blocks, they suddenly tossed him a gun and said, "Are you in? We're robbing that guy who's been selling on our turf; he's right up the street." Not really wanting to take part but eager to share in the proceeds, he sat tight. His "act of conscience" was to set the safety lock on the gun so there would be no chance of his ever firing it. When the car came to a screeching halt at the rival's corner, he got out of the car with everyone else and held his gun in the air. Unfortunately, the other guy pulled out *his* gun and everyone started firing. My client jumped back in the car and fled.

When I first saw him, he was adamant about fighting the case: He was no murderer. He couldn't let go of the fact that *he was just going to the store.* He admitted being with the others, having the gun, and getting out of the car gun in hand, but believed that he had sufficiently separated himself by putting the safety on the gun. He said the police would verify that the gun, which he had abandoned, was never fired. It took time—not too much, because the first to offer testimony against the ringleader would get the best plea deal—but I managed to get the client to see the truth of his situation: By taking up arms along with the others, he had made himself an accessory to murder. Although he didn't mean for it to happen, felt terrible for the young man's family, and did not want to go to prison, he needed to cut his losses and negotiate a plea.

Though we may embellish, exaggerate, and omit in the course of advocacy—consistent with ethical rules and standards—within the lawyer-client relationship, criminal lawyers tend to be compulsive truth tellers.

⁓

It is hard to say whether Scholl's decision to portray Kelly as heterosexual was the strategy that ultimately doomed her before the jury. The prosecution could then have it both ways: Kelly was a devoted girlfriend who did Billy Ronald's bidding; and Kelly was strange, different, deviant, a woman who would travel and live with a man but also play around with women. It would have been simpler and more believable for Kelly to tell the truth: She was and is a lesbian; she and Billy Ronald were never intimately involved; she had a girlfriend that summer and Billy Ronald had a boyfriend.

Kelly is an essentially honest person. At the time of trial, she had never before lied about the one thing that some gays and lesbians routinely conceal. She lacked the sophistication that good liars possess. She was probably not credible when she testified that she had "dated" Billy Ronald and was not a "practicing lesbian." No doubt this hurt her before the jury. In a murder case, where the question is whether you helped commit a savage crime, being a liar is probably worse than being a lesbian. If Kelly could lie to a jury about who she was, she could be lying about the rest. It is also hard to say what motivated Scholl's view that Kelly's lesbianism would hurt her more than being portrayed as Billy Ronald's partner: Was it a reflection of his own fears and prejudices or an accurate assessment of an Oneida County jury in 1977?

Kelly never felt that Scholl was troubled by her sexual orientation. When she told him that she was gay, he didn't seem bothered. This was consistent with Scholl's view of himself: He was liberal and proud of it. He had been an early supporter of the civil rights movement. He had no problem with women's liberation or gay liberation. He had been a staunch opponent of the Vietnam War. One of his proudest moments was meeting John F. Kennedy when he was campaigning for president. Kennedy had been handing out *PT 109* tie tacks and gave one to Scholl. Scholl kept it his whole life.

But the year of the trial was a banner year for the anti–gay rights movement. This was the year that Florida orange juice spokeswoman Anita Bryant launched her successful crusade against gay rights. In 1977 Florida's Dade County (now Miami-

Dade) passed a human rights ordinance that prohibited discrimination on the basis of sexual orientation. In response, Bryant and "Save Our Children," one of the first organizations of a newly galvanized religious right, conducted a highly publicized campaign to repeal the ordinance, calling homosexuality a sin and warning of the threat of homosexual recruitment of children. Bryant's campaign led to the repeal of the Miami antidiscrimination ordinance by a substantial margin and sparked the spread of antigay sentiment in the rest of the country. Sometimes this sentiment turned violent. In June 1977 a gay San Franciscan named Robert Hillsborough was stabbed to death only steps from his home by four young men proclaiming "This one's for Anita Bryant."

Perhaps John Scholl was mindful of the goings-on in Florida. Bryant's campaign had garnered national attention. If Miami, a relatively enlightened place, bought Bryant's antigay rhetoric, it didn't bode well for more conservative Oneida County.

But there is a paradox here for Kelly as well. Some might find it a disturbing inconsistency. Why would Kelly, who felt so strongly about the truth that she was willing to risk a life sentence for it, go along with this lie? She had never before felt a moment's shame or embarrassment about being gay, but was now putting her hand on a Bible and denying it. Was this a lesser truth that could be sacrificed in view of the larger truth of her innocence?

Kelly says that she was only doing what her lawyer advised. She wasn't happy about it, but she felt that Scholl knew best.

ᕼ

There is a deeper paradox. Despite the system's theoretical interest in protecting people who are innocent, no one in the system thinks they will ever encounter one. Busy urban courthouses have their hands full processing the guilty. Injecting a truthful, factually innocent person into the criminal system throws a wrench in the works.

One of my favorite stories about the problem of innocence in ordinary criminal practice comes from James Kunen's memoir, *How Can You Defend Those People?* Kunen, a former Washington, D.C. public defender, begins the book with a story from when he was a student in NYU's criminal defense clinic. His first client, Judy Hoffman, was a "gumcracking 18-year-old in platform shoes, tight jeans, a slinky jersey and pink sunglasses" who was charged with loitering for purposes of prostitution in Manhattan. The undercover police officer who arrested her had no doubt about Judy's occupation when he saw her in the late evening dressed as she was. But Kunen learned the truth from his client: After having dinner at her cousin's house, Judy and her boyfriend drove to a Midtown disco, where the boyfriend dropped Judy off while he looked for parking. She had just bought cigarettes and was about to call her sister from a payphone when the undercover officer came up behind her and told her she was under arrest. When Judy said, "What do you mean?" He replied, "You're a whore."

In court, everyone—the prosecutor, judge, and court staff—assumed Judy was guilty. After all, asks Kunen, why would New York's finest arrest a young woman for no reason at all? Kunen was immediately pressured by the other institutional actors to get his client to take a plea that would lead to the dismissal of charges after a short period of probation. The judge was unhappy when Kunen balked. What could Kunen want other than what had been offered? This was a run-of-the-mill case that needed to be disposed of quickly. But Kunen wouldn't do it. When the judge, plainly annoyed, finally asked why not, Kunen managed to blurt out the answer: "But she isn't a prostitute, Your Honor." The judge said, "Oh well, in that case, she can go. Case dismissed."[2]

If there is any doubt that the system is not really interested in the factually innocent, one need look no further than U.S. Supreme Court decisions limiting the right to habeas corpus review. In the 1993 case *Herrera v. Collins,*[3] the Court denied access to the federal courts to a death row inmate who had evidence of actual innocence. The Court ruled that "errors of fact" are not a proper basis for habeas review even if an innocent person might be executed as a result of these errors.

At trial, too, the truth—even if it supports a claim of innocence—is not always helpful. Sometimes the truth is wildly implausible, well beyond the Kunen story. I learned this early on in my own public defender days. During the training programs, one of the senior lawyers shared a story. He was representing a man who had denied committing a series of thefts. The man claimed that an enormous talking chicken had done it. The lawyer thought the client had a mental health problem and referred the case to the office's social services division for evaluation. Fortunately, he also asked an investigator to look into it. After some digging around, the investigator discovered that on the day of the thefts, there had been a promotional event for a newly opened fast food restaurant specializing in fried chicken. As part of the event, the restaurant had hired a man to wear a bright yellow chicken suit and hand out flyers. Several witnesses confirmed that they saw this "chicken-man" in possession of the stolen items near where the thefts had occurred.

I understood this anecdote to be a broad institutional lesson, the sort that gives rise to a number of maxims: Truth is stranger than fiction, don't be too quick to judge, you never know, and, most important, investigation is central to good defense work. I also understood it to suggest that the truth may not always be the most convincing or credible story. Stories need to be viscerally persuasive. They need to ring true.

Criminal lawyers have a utilitarian relationship to the truth. To the extent the truth is useful—as it was with the chicken-man—criminal lawyers use it. But they are not hamstrung by it. When it doesn't serve, they reject it.

Another favorite story about the occasional and surprising usefulness of truth comes from a lawyer named Barry Winston. Winston was representing a young man accused of car theft. The police had attempted to stop the car in which the accused was riding for a traffic violation, but the car sped away. A chase ensued, during which a record check was conducted and the car came up stolen. The chase came to a halt when the fleeing car careened out of control and flipped over. Fortunately, no one was seriously hurt. But Winston's client, who was alleged to be the driver, was arrested. Upon inspecting the car, the police found that the car's steering column had been broken and a screwdriver was in the ignition.

At trial, the police stuck to their police report. They described their attempts to stop the car, the driver's failure to stop when signaled to do so, the ensuing flight, the dramatic end, and their apprehension of the accused. They identified the accused as the driver of the car, who had emerged from the front left seat, and described the state of the steering column and ignition. The inference was that the driver of the car knew it had been stolen because of the presence of a screwdriver in addition to the driver's flight.

On cross-examination, Winston emphasized the fact that the police had seen his client emerge from the front left seat of the car. He encouraged the police in their certainty of this fact and established the connection between their certainty about his client's placement in the car with their identification of him as the driver. He said to the testifying officer, "That's how you knew he was the driver: He emerged from the left side of the car." The officers agreed.

In his closing argument, Winston pointed out that with the car *upside down,* the person emerging from the left front seat would be the passenger, not the driver. His client was acquitted.[4]

Given the defense lawyer's casual relationship to truth, there is a stunning change of perspective when a lawyer represents an innocent person. Suddenly there is nothing more important than the truth, nothing more sacred. Now the lawyer who is ordinarily indifferent to the truth is plagued by it and outraged that the *system* is indifferent to it. The lawyer who usually decries the murkiness of truth now sees it in neon clarity. The lawyer who has come to feel philosophically estranged from the truth now embraces it.

The incongruity of this turnabout can be hard to reconcile. You get used to thinking of the truth as something of a nuisance. You get used to shrugging it off, playing it down, making light of it. Now you're on your high horse. You hardly recognize yourself.

Lawyers with innocent clients can become downright desperate about the truth. Gone is the irreverence, the cynicism. They wear their hearts on their sleeves. They become humble and, worse, supplicants. "Please," they beseech police officers, prosecutors, judges. "My client is *innocent.*" Now they are willing to divulge information they would never ordinarily divulge—witness statements, client statements, holes in the prosecution's case that might be more effectively exploited at trial—in order to convince those with power that the client has been wrongly accused. Of course, the problem with the defender's newfound embrace of truth is that it is no simpler when a client is innocent than when she is guilty. The truth, even when it supports innocence, is as obscure as ever. It is also no less prey to distortion, only this time it's the prosecutor doing the shaping. What's good for the goose is good for the gander: Prosecutors can be just as clever as defense lawyers at slapping down the truth and making it appear otherwise.

The truth can also be downright unconvincing, no matter how utterly *true* it may be. For some innocent defendants, it may be more of a hindrance than a help. As writer Janet Malcolm has observed:

> The truth is messy, incoherent, aimless, boring, absurd. The truth does not make a good story; that's why we have art. The prosecutor prosecuting an innocent person or the defense lawyer defending a guilty client actually have an easier task than their opposite numbers. In the unjust prosecution and in the lying defense, much of the work of narration—of transforming messy actuality in to an orderly story—has already been done. The just prosecution and the defense of an innocent require a great deal more work. For truth to prevail at trial, it must be laboriously transformed into a kind of travesty of itself.[5]

The prosecution's case against Kelly rested heavily on their lone eyewitness, a man named Robert Hyland, who had his own truth.

Hyland had been a night watchman at the Oneida Limited Silver Flatware plant, just down the road from the Seaway station. He was 59 at the time of the crime and in his 60s by the time of trial.

He had never been involved in the criminal justice system and was not happy to be a witness. He was not someone who sought the public light. Yet this was a big crime; it had been in all the papers. He wished it had been someone else at the Seaway that day.

When Hyland was interviewed by the police on August 13, two days after the crime, he said that he had driven into the station at approximately 12:50 P.M. and parked next to the gas pumps on the side nearest the road. Since no attendant was in view, Hyland got out of his car and stood for a minute or two behind his car. (These were the days before self-service pumps.) As he was waiting, a car came from the west side of the station and pulled up to the pump on the side nearest the building. When the police asked him to describe the driver, Hyland said, "I am not sure, but I believe the operator was a white female. She had long black shoulder length hair and was wearing dark clothing. . . . The type of hairstyle that this person had did not allow me to see her face. . . . I had never seen the girl or the car before."

According to Hyland, after the car pulled up and "a few seconds had elapsed," he saw a white male emerge from the station and approach Hyland's car. The man, whom Hyland described in some detail, asked which car was first. Hyland said he could pump either car, and the man indicated that he would take care of Hyland first. Hyland then asked for $5.00 worth of gasoline, and the man pumped the gas for him, at all times holding the nozzle of the hose. While this was happening, Hyland and the man engaged in "general conversation about the weather." When the requested amount had been pumped, Hyland got in his car and left. He told the police that he "did not pay any attention as to what service [the man] offered the other car." By Hyland's estimate, he left the station at 12:55 P.M.

Based on Hyland's description of the man who pumped gas for him, police sketch artists were able to prepare and circulate a sketch of the man. No such sketch was made of the person in the other car at the Seaway station.

Following the preparation of the sketch, the police did not contact Hyland again until December 1975, 28 months after the murder. At that time, a police officer who had been involved in the investigation came to Hyland's home with two photo spreads. He first displayed a set of photographs of males from which Hyland selected a photo of Billy Ronald Kelly as the man who had pumped gas for him.

The officer then gave Hyland a set of 12 photographs of women. It is not clear why the officer assembled a female-only photo spread in view of Hyland's less than certain statement about the gender of the person in the other car. His description of the person could well have applied to a young man with long hair. In 1973, long hair for men was the fashion. My own 1974 high school yearbook features page after page of boys with shoulder-length hair. Probably the police never considered including both men and women in the photo spread for the driver once they determined that Billy Ronald was the perpetrator and Kelly his companion. Once the police linked Kelly with Billy Ronald, they had who they were looking for.

No doubt the officer who showed Hyland the photos had this well in mind.

Of the photos shown to Hyland, eight were unmarked, three were marked "New York State Police," and one had the notation "Sheriff Department." Hyland initially selected two photographs, each of a different woman, and both of which had law enforcement notations. He ultimately signed the back of one—a photograph of

Kelly with a sheriff's department insignia—later saying that he selected this photograph because it was "possibly" the person who had driven the other car at the gas station. But the second photograph "looked like" the driver too.

No one knows exactly what the police said to Hyland when they showed him the photos. The police report offers only a brief summary of what went on.

Three months later Hyland appeared before a grand jury where he offered testimony similar to his original police statement. He said the driver "looked like a female." When asked whether he could positively identify the photograph of Kelly as the driver of the car, he said, "I can't say positive [but] . . . it was the same style hair, long hair." The best he could say was that it "could be" the person he saw at the station but he "couldn't say for sure."

In January 1977, 41 months after the crime, Hyland had one final opportunity before trial to talk about whom he had seen at the Seaway station. At a suppression hearing, at which Scholl sought to keep out Hyland's identification on the grounds that it was the product of police suggestion and not reliable, Hyland recounted his earlier photo selections. He admitted seeing the sheriff and police markings on some of the photos. He said he narrowed it down to two photos because both looked like the person he had seen. He ultimately selected Kelly's photo because she was "possibly" the one. Although Kelly was seated next to her lawyer at counsel table, at no time did Hyland identify her as the person he had seen in the car that day. Hyland's only reference to Kelly was to contrast her appearance with that of the person he had seen, saying that the one at the Seaway had "long, darker hair . . . than the one that's right there, now." He looked right at Kelly but never said it was her.

Apart from describing hair color and length, Hyland did not offer any other physical characteristics of the driver until asked by the defense whether he could say how tall the person was. Hyland said he had never seen the driver outside of the car, but he would estimate at least as tall as he was and "maybe a little bit taller." Hyland was five foot seven. Kelly is five foot two.

Trial began on March 14, 1977, more than three and a half years after the murder. At trial, the only evidence that Kelly was there on the day of the murder was Robert Hyland's testimony. No other witness claimed to have seen Kelly at the station, or anyone resembling her. The prosecutor knew that Hyland was critical to his case and conferred with him just before he took the stand. In this conference, he showed Hyland the photographs of Kelly and Billy Ronald that Hyland had selected in December 1975. He pointed out that these were the two defendants now on trial and urged Hyland to be strong and "stick to [his] guns."

Hyland then took the stand and, for the first time, positively identified Kelly as the person who was in the other car. When pressed by Scholl, Hyland insisted that he was certain that the driver was female because of the way she used a comb that she retrieved from a brown and gold handbag. Notwithstanding his prior sworn statement, he now claimed that he had seen the driver's cheeks, nose, eyes, and forehead. This was the basis on which he had selected Kelly's photo and now identified her in court. Although he conceded that he had spent no more than five minutes at the station, that the man came to pump his gas within seconds of his arrival, that he focused his attention much more on the man pumping gas than the person in the car, and that he paid more attention to the car itself than the person in it because he "was impressed with its finish," he maintained it was Kelly who had been in the car.

Hyland claimed that any inconsistencies between his trial testimony and his statement two days after the crime were the result of poor police drafting or his not having read the statement carefully before signing it.

~

Erroneous eyewitness identifications, made in good faith, are a major cause of wrongful convictions in the United States.[6] As Justice William Brennan once noted, "The vagaries of eyewitness identification are well known; the annals of criminal law are rife with instances of mistaken identification."[7] Prominent English barrister and Cambridge University professor Glanville Williams added his own observation: "In England and America most of the spectacular miscarriages of justice have been due to wrong identification of the defendant as a culprit."[8]

The annals to which Justice Brennan referred must now include the majority of the more than 200 postconviction DNA exonerations that have occurred in the United States.[9] In three-fourths of these exonerations, the key factor behind the wrongful conviction was sincere, confident, but mistaken eyewitness identification.[10] As DNA is not available or relevant in most cases, but eyewitness testimony plays a regular part, it is likely that many innocent people have been convicted based on the testimony of a mistaken witness.

The problem of misidentification has long been recognized. In 1909 Harvard psychology professor Hugo Munsterberg challenged the reliability of eyewitness testimony in his influential book *On the Witness Stand.*[11] In 1932 Yale law professor Edwin Borchard chronicled 65 instances of wrongful convictions, including

29 stories of misidentification, in his equally important book, *Convicting the Innocent: Errors of Criminal Justice.*[12] The stories largely involve well-meaning witnesses who believed in the accuracy of their mistaken identifications.

One of the best-known wrongful identification cases in recent years involves another North Carolina woman named Jennifer Thompson. Thompson was a 22-year-old college student in Burlington, North Carolina, when, in 1984, a man broke into her apartment and raped her at knifepoint. Thompson gave a detailed description of her attacker and helped a police artist develop a composite sketch. She picked a suspect out of a series of photographs, and again in a lineup. She felt sure the man she selected, Ronald Cotton, was her rapist. She could not have been more confident. At trial, she maintained her certainty. She identified Cotton. The jury quickly convicted. [13]

Cotton's lawyer had endeavored at trial to call an expert witness on eyewitness identification, but the judge said no, it was a matter of common sense. The appeals court agreed, holding that the effects of stress, cross-racial factors (Thompson was white, her attacker black), and the frailty of memory were commonly known to jurors.[14] Cotton was sentenced to life in prison.

Eleven years later Thompson learned that Cotton was not her attacker. Instead, it was a man named Bobby Poole, a serial rapist serving a life sentence who had bragged about raping her. Although at first Thompson did not believe it—when confronted with Poole in court, Thompson said she had never seen him before—DNA evidence confirmed it was Poole.

After Cotton's exoneration and release from prison, Thompson befriended him. Remarkably, Cotton bore her no ill will. Thompson, however, could not let herself off so easily. In a *New*

York Times op-ed, she described her "constant anguish" over having sent an innocent man to prison for more than a decade.[15]

Thompson has since become an advocate for criminal justice reform, urging changes in identification procedures so that what happened to Ronald Cotton won't happen to others.

Eyewitness identifications have great potential to cause wrongful convictions because of the powerful impact they have on a range of institutional actors in the criminal justice system. One social scientist, commenting on the "pivotal role" that eyewitness testimony plays in criminal cases, describes how eyewitness testimony influences the legal process even before the case goes to trial:

> If there is an eyewitness, especially one who makes a positive impression, the police and prosecutor's office are more likely to pursue a case. And what the witness reports will influence the course of an investigation. When we add to these facts the research evidence that eyewitness memory is often inaccurate, we have a real potential for frequent misfires of the justice process, errors that cost money, time, and, in some cases, the freedom of an innocent person.[16]

But the impact of eyewitness testimony is especially powerful on juries. For many jurors, the case is over when a credible witness identifies the accused with certainty.[17] The Second Circuit, which ruled against Kelly, has recognized the powerful prejudicial impact of this testimony, especially where there is a violent crime:

> [J]uries, naturally desirous to punish a vicious crime, may well be unschooled in the effects that the subtle compound of suggestion, anxiety, and forgetfulness in the face of the need to recall often has on witnesses. Accordingly, doubts over the strength of the evidence of a defendant's guilt may be resolved on the basis of the eyewitness' seeming certainty when he

points to the defendant and exclaims with conviction that veils all doubt, "[T]hat's the man!"[18]

Yet a 2004 study conducted by the Public Defender Service for the District of Columbia and University of California at Irvine professor Elizabeth Loftus, a nationally recognized expert on identification, found that jurors frequently misunderstand how memory works and overestimate eyewitness reliability. Of the nearly 1,000 prospective jurors surveyed, a substantial number overestimated the ability of people to remember strangers' faces, especially members of other races. Most placed unwarranted trust in the identification abilities of police officers and did not understand how police procedures can affect the accuracy of identification.[19]

The study confirmed what Professor Loftus said 20 years ago: "[C]ommon beliefs held by people regarding eyewitness ability [do] not always conform to the findings from psychological research."[20]

A common and troubling misperception, confirmed by the Public Defender Service study, is that the more confident or certain a witness is, the more accurate the testimony is likely to be. In fact, research suggests that there is little relationship between confidence and accuracy, especially when the opportunity to observe was poor or fleeting.[21]

In response to the problem of unreliable identification, many commentators have recommended that courts allow expert testimony on the psychology of memory and identification. Typically, an expert would debunk myths by explaining that witness confidence is not an indicator of accuracy, accuracy of memory declines over time, and memory is not an exact, videotape-like recollection of events.[22] Such an expert witness might describe how an eyewitness's trial testimony could be the product of multiple sources of information that have melded together in the witness's mind over time. As Professor Loftus has written: "Post-event information can not only enhance existing memories but also change a witness's memory and cause nonexistent details to become incorporated into a previously acquired memory."[23]

Indeed, Robert Hyland's trial memory was substantially different from his previously recounted memory. Not only was he surer about what he had seen, but he suddenly added details that he had never offered before. Unlike Hyland's previous statements that he had seen no one at the station when he arrived, he testified at trial that he had seen a man and a woman between the gas pumps and the building. According to Hyland, the man entered the building and he did not notice where the woman went. He then recounted the appearance of a blue car from around the corner of the building and specifically identified Kelly as the person driving the car. Unlike his statement two days after the crime—that he could not see the face of the driver—at trial Hyland said he saw the driver's cheeks, nose, eyes, and forehead.

Scholl never consulted or tried to call an expert witness on the fallibility of eyewitness identification. He probably thought the trial judge would not have allowed such evidence. When the jury convicted Kelly on March 29, 1977, it conveyed its belief in Robert Hyland's testimony.

⌒

At trial, the prosecution called 25 witnesses in addition to Robert Hyland. Their testimony established that Billy Ronald and Kelly traveled together from High Point to Utica in Kelly's blue Road

Runner. Before arriving in Utica, they stayed in nearby Herkimer, New York. Then they moved into a rooming house on Rutger Street, where they remained until mid-August. While in Utica, Billy Ronald worked on a construction site and often drove Kelly's car. There was testimony that Billy Ronald and Kelly spent time at the local gay bar, the Hub, and Billy Ronald had a relationship with a man he met there named William Sullivan.

Much of the testimony emphasized the fact that Billy Ronald and Kelly had traveled to the area together. They shared living quarters, finances, and a car, and they both left town a week or two after the crime. Two surprise witnesses were flown in from North Carolina to testify. One witness claimed that Kelly had told him that she loved Billy Ronald and would "lie, die, or go to hell" for him. Another witness said that Kelly had admitted coloring her hair that summer so that it was darker than usual.

There was disturbing testimony by a man and his teenage daughter. The man dropped his daughter off at the Seaway station shortly after 1:00 P.M. He had done this many times before because the daughter was friendly with Hatch and liked to help him pump gas. When the girl did not see Hatch outside at the station, she filled in for him for a couple of cars. Then she went looking for him. She found his dead body on the back room floor, his throat slashed, blood everywhere.

It turns out that the girl was more than friendly with Hatch: She was his girlfriend, and she was the first to discover his body.

The Seaway district manager determined that $279.00 was missing from the cash register. Scholl called a few incidental witnesses, but his case rested primarily on Kelly's testimony. Kelly's truth—and her ability to convey it—was the only thing that could rebut Hyland's truth and the innuendo underlying the rest of the state's case. Kelly was not on the stand long. She testified that she had met Billy Ronald in 1972 and driven to New York with him the next summer. She said that Billy Ronald had the use of her car during the week and on weekends, occasionally overnight. She and Billy Ronald were in Utica for around six weeks. They left when her money ran out. Her father wired her $40 for the trip home.

Kelly readily acknowledged that she was in Utica on the day of the murder but denied any knowledge of it. Because it was so long ago, she could not say exactly what she had been doing at the time of the crime. She guessed she would have been sleeping late, drinking coffee, or playing softball. She denied ever owning a handbag; she carried her wallet in her pocket. She denied ever having dyed her hair or telling anyone that she had done so. She denied having said to anyone that she loved Billy Ronald or would lie or die for him. She never said such a thing and never would.

She told the jury that she didn't know why people had said things about her that weren't true. All she knew was she had nothing to do with this terrible crime. She was not the person in the car. She was innocent.

Kelly's former girlfriend Gerri did not testify. She had no memory of Kelly's whereabouts on that August day. She did not appreciate being questioned by the police or investigators about her private life, especially in connection with a murder. She found the police hostile and threatening. She had had a summer romance nearly four years before, but it was a distant memory. She did not want to be involved. Scholl saw no reason to push her.

Billy Ronald did not testify and called no witnesses.

∽

Since Kelly's conviction, there has been a considerable change in thinking about the forensic techniques of eyewitness identification. At the time of the Hatch murder investigation, there were no clear nationwide guidelines for conducting lineups and photo spreads. Police were trained according to local practices. In 1998 a group of social scientists published a best practices guide to help reduce the risk of misidentification.[24] Many state and local law enforcement agencies have reevaluated their procedures in light of it.

The federal government has also shown an increased concern. In 1995 the U.S. Department of Justice acknowledged that eyewitness misidentification played a major role in the vast majority of the DNA exoneration cases.[25] In 1999 the National Institute of Justice published a report exploring the development of improved procedures for collecting and preserving eyewitness evidence in the criminal justice system. The report recognized that current scientific knowledge could be used to improve the reliability of eyewitness identification.[26]

A substantial body of literature exists on interviewers unintentionally conveying information to subjects, which is known as the experimenter expectancy effect. The "double-blind administration" —having an officer who knows nothing be in charge of the identification process and letting the witness know the officer knows nothing—prevents intentional and unintentional suggestiveness. An officer who knows nothing won't be able to suggest verbally ("I noticed you paused on number 4") or nonverbally (lingering longer on one "filler" or photo, raised eyebrows, change of posture, change in voice tone) who the suspect is. It also prevents postprocedure feedback ("Good job." "That's who we think did it." "Congratulations!").[27]

The need for blind testing procedures in scientific research is so widely accepted that respected journals usually refuse to publish experiments in which the interviewer knew the desired outcome.

Studies have also shown that it is essential for the investigator to warn an eyewitness that the suspect may or may not be present in the lineup or photo spread. Otherwise, witnesses will assume that the culprit is there and that his or her task is to pick someone, anyone—as if it were a multiple choice exam, and "none of the above" is not one of the choices. By not mentioning that the suspect might not be present, there is an inherent suggestion that he or she *is* present.[28]

The other significant development in the forensics of eyewitness identification is the preference for "sequential" lineups and photo spreads over "simultaneous" ones. Research has shown that, when compared to the traditional simultaneous procedure, showing lineup members or photos one at a time produces a substantially lower rate of mistaken identifications. Again, instead of making a relative or comparative judgment—picking the person who most resembles the perpetrator—the witness makes an absolute judgment. In a sequential lineup the witness considers a single face and compares it not to an array of choices but to his or her own memory of the culprit.[29]

There has been resistance to instituting these reforms even though they require no additional effort or cost. Some law enforcement agencies have tried to counter proposed identification reforms by producing their own studies. A 2006 study by the Illinois State Police, for example, found that sequential lineups made witnesses less likely to choose anyone, and more likely to choose an innocent person standing in as a "filler." By contrast, witnesses in traditional police lineups were more likely to identify the suspect.[30] But critics argue that the study is flawed because of how it was conducted.[31]

Meanwhile, a small number of jurisdictions, including the state of New Jersey, Hennepin County, Minnesota (where Minneapolis is located), and the city of Boston have made significant changes in their identification procedures.[32] As of 2008, nine states—Georgia, Illinois, North Carolina, New Mexico, Texas, Vermont, West Virginia, Wisconsin, and Virginia—were either exploring or implementing new protocols.[33] Notwithstanding the Illinois police study, the U.S. Department of Justice recommends sequential lineups over simultaneous lineups because of greater accuracy.[34]

Anita Bryant's antigay campaign was not the only prominent event at the time of the trial. In January 1977, two months before trial, newly inaugurated President Jimmy Carter pardoned Vietnam War draft evaders. The next month President Carter appeared on television in a cardigan sweater to urge Americans to conserve energy during the "oil crisis." Later that year Amnesty International won the Nobel Peace Prize for protecting the rights of political prisoners, the U.S. Supreme Court ruled that there was no right to Medicaid-funded abortions, South African Steve Biko died of injuries sustained while in police custody, and the New York Yankees beat the Los Angeles Dodgers in six games in the World Series. Elvis Presley, Groucho Marx, Bing Crosby, and Charlie Chaplin all died in 1977. So did Anaïs Nin and Vladimir Nabokov.

In 1977 people flocked to theaters to see a previously un-known actor named Sylvester Stallone play a struggling boxer in the film *Rocky* and to see George Lukas's very first *Star Wars* film. This was also the year that Woody Allen finally won the Best Picture Academy Award for *Annie Hall*. Popular television shows included *Laverne & Shirley, Happy Days, Three's Company,* and *60 Minutes*. Alex Haley's *Roots* and Colleen McCullough's *The Thorn Birds* were best-sellers.

The trial was held in Utica, the county seat of Oneida County. But jurors would come from the entire county, which included the city of Rome to the west, Utica to the east, some affluent outlying suburbs, and a number of smaller, rural townships. Oneida is among the most rural of the 62 counties in New York State. At the time, the biggest employers in the county were General Electric, Utica Linens, the sheet metal manufacturing company Bosserts, and the Oneida Limited Silver Flatware plant, which was just down the road from the Seaway station on Route 5. For leisure, people in the area might go for clams and beer at Spilka's Hotel in downtown Utica, see a hockey game (Utica had its own team, and the Paul Newman film *Slapshot* was filmed in the city the same year as the trial), or play the horses at the Vernon Downs racetrack. In warm weather, the Route 49 Drive-In was a popular destination.

Politically and socially, Oneida County is conservative. Except for Utica, a Democratic stronghold since World War II, it is reliably Republican. In the 1976 presidential election, which occurred only a few months before the trial, Oneida county voters backed incumbent Gerald Ford—who took office after Richard Nixon resigned over the Watergate scandal—over "reform" candidate Jimmy Carter. More recently, in the 2000 and 2004 presidential elections, Oneida County voted decisively for George W. Bush over both Al Gore and John Kerry.

It would not be fair to say the entire area is strictly conservative, however. Several nearby colleges and universities provide a liberal influence and a regular influx of young people. Still, prospective Oneida County jurors in 1977 were likely to be white, Catholic, working class, high school educated, and of Italian, Irish, or German descent. There would have been relatively few blacks as the percentage of African Americans in Oneida County has seldom risen above 6 percent. Although the county was named after the Oneida Indians, scarcely 500 Native Americans lived there as of 2000, so it is unlikely there were any in the jury pool.

Violent crime, especially murder, is a rarity in Oneida County. In 1977, the year of the trial, there were no murders in all of Oneida County and fewer than 30 robberies. Although crime has gotten worse in recent years, there were only 10 murders in the entire county in 2000.

Murders never happen in Sherrill. The Hatch murder was an extraordinary event.

It is likely that, in 1977, most residents of Oneida County would not have known many openly gay people. It would have been a fair guess that most people would tend to side with law enforcement. But Scholl would have to know more about individual jurors in order to determine what they would make of Kelly's sexuality (and whether they could critically examine Hyland's in-court identification as well). He would have to know who they were, what sort of life experiences they had, and what attitudes and values they held. Probing questions during jury selection would have been the only way to uncover whether the jurors would be prejudiced against Kelly simply because she was a lesbian, and also whether they were able to put the state to its burden of proof.[35]

But Scholl asked no questions about the jurors' views on homosexuality. Once he determined that Kelly's lesbianism was a liability, he saw no reason to inquire into what jurors might have thought about it.

Although jurors usually try hard to put aside their prejudices and render a verdict based only on the evidence, Kelly's jury was never given the opportunity to grapple with theirs. Scholl left them no choice but to believe that Kelly and Billy Ronald were sexual and criminal partners. No wonder they believed Kelly was at the station that day.

Since no transcript was made of jury selection, we don't know what questions Scholl posed to prospective jurors about eyewitness fallibility or the burden of proof in a criminal case.

When the weather was starting to change and she ran out of money, it was time for Kelly to go home. She missed her family and needed to go back to work. She thought that Billy Ronald might decide to stay longer and catch a bus home, but he said he might as well go with her. With the money her father had sent, she and Billy Ronald headed south.

Unbeknownst to Kelly, she was riding with a killer.

Then came another complicating truth.

On the way back to North Carolina, Billy Ronald robbed and killed another gas station attendant, this time in Virginia. The evidence was clear. And for this murder, Kelly was undeniably present.

Here's what happened, according to both Kelly and the Virginia police:

Billy Ronald did most of the driving on the way back home. Kelly wasn't feeling well because of a heavy menstrual cycle. She had taken some Midol—an over-the-counter drug that can cause drowsiness—and slept for most of the trip. On August 26, not far from the North Carolina border, she was awakened by the sound of a car backfiring. They were at a gas station, and Billy Ronald was not in the car. He came back visibly agitated. He seemed to have cut his hand. When Kelly asked him what was going on, he told her to shut up and mind her own business. Still groggy from medication, she did as she was told and went back to sleep.

It did not remotely occur to Kelly that Billy Ronald could be a killer. Such an idea would never have popped into her mind. To the extent she gave it any thought, she figured Billy Ronald was in a bad mood. Maybe he was tired from doing all the driving, maybe he got into an argument at the station. She had no idea how he got cut; it was a mishap of some sort. She did not think for one second that Billy Ronald had done something *criminal*.

When two Virginia state police officers contacted Kelly some months later, she had to confront the truth. That sound she had heard at the gas station was not a car backfiring, it was a gunshot. Although Kelly had never seen Billy Ronald with a gun, he had apparently shot and killed a gas station attendant during a robbery just outside of Danville, Virginia. Kelly responded to what the officers told her by cooperating fully with them, telling them all she knew, and agreeing to testify against Billy Ronald.

Kelly struggled to accept that she had been in the car—and had spent several weeks—with someone who turned out to be an armed madman.

Kelly's assistance was critical to Billy Ronald's prosecution in Virginia, and local police and prosecutors were happy to have it. As a result of Kelly's help, Billy Ronald pled guilty to murder and received a 35-year sentence. The Virginia authorities did not prosecute Kelly. What's more, they never considered prosecuting her. They believed that her presence at the scene was unwitting and that she had been exploited and deceived by Billy Ronald. Looking back, this is astonishing. Not known for lenience, Virginia authorities would never take the word of someone they suspected of criminal involvement. Second only to Texas in the number of death sentences handed down, Virginia prides itself on being tough on crime.

Still, some might wonder how Kelly could have been so blind to Billy Ronald's character. How could she have spent so much time with him and not have recognized the killer—the *psychopath*—in him? After all, she had known Billy Ronald in North Carolina, had spent hours with him on the road, and had shared quarters in Utica. It seems unlikely that Kelly had no clue during all that time that Billy Ronald had killed and robbed *twice,* once with a knife and once with a gun.

She had no clue because Billy Ronald was a charlatan. By the time Kelly met him, he had already fooled a lot of people and would continue to do so.

Billy Ronald was not the sweet-natured, fun-loving country boy Kelly thought he was. He was an accomplished con man. Before he met Kelly in 1972, Billy Ronald had been living in Virginia. More precisely, he had been living in a cell in the Virginia State Penitentiary, where he was serving a sentence for burglary, larceny, and tax fraud. He had also served time for the "felonious possession of hacksaw blades" for having a hacksaw at the Pittsylvania County Jail. These were not his first run-ins with the law.

While he was serving time for the Virginia murder, and before he was accused of the New York crime, he killed again. Although the records are sketchy, it appears that Billy Ronald and another inmate killed a third inmate. As there is no record of a conviction for any offense connected to this incident, Billy Ronald was either acquitted at trial—perhaps on the grounds of self-defense—or the charges were dismissed.

Even after Billy Ronald was a twice-convicted murderer serving two sentences in Virginia and New York, he continued his career as a con artist. In 1992, while in prison, Billy Ronald was convicted in Loudon County, Virginia, of being the mastermind behind an elaborate scheme to file phony state tax returns, bilking the government of almost $30,000 in refunds. The scheme was so clever that even the attorney who prosecuted Billy Ronald called it a "neat little trick," and a former IRS investigator who headed the criminal investigation unit of the Virginia Department of Taxation called it "ingenious."[36]

Under Billy Ronald's direction, a group of convicted prisoners prepared W–2 forms, used the names of other inmates and prison officials on tax returns, and printed envelopes with the return address of a circuit court judge to get refund checks into the prison undetected. One of the inmate's mothers helped to launder the money. The scheme started in 1988, when Billy Ronald was in Mecklenburg Prison in southern Virginia. He and the others filed at least 36 phony tax returns and cashed $11,000 in checks. Although neither Billy Ronald nor his fellow prisoners had a background in accounting, the scam was well conceived and executed. The only reason they were caught is because Billy Ronald was transferred to a different prison where, as luck would have it, there was another inmate named Billy R. Kelly. This caused prison officials to monitor their mail more carefully, and they eventually uncovered the con.

If Billy Ronald could fool the State of Virginia for four years from behind bars, Kelly was easy pickings.

~

The New York police had their own truth.

Between 1973 and 1975—before they learned of the Virginia murder—the police combed the area for suspects. They brought in dozens of people for questioning. Some were given polygraph exams. Some were fingerprinted. Some were shown to eyewitness Robert Hyland.

A Syracuse man with a criminal record who had spent the night of August 10, 1973, at a Sherrill motel with a female companion was the first to be questioned. He denied any knowledge of the crime and passed a polygraph exam. His girlfriend corroborated his story. Two men from Orlando, Florida, who had been driving a blue 1966 Ford and were arrested for disorderly conduct in Binghamton, New York, were questioned. Both denied ever being in Sherrill and passed polygraph exams. Two local men who were seen driving a greenish blue Ford in Oneida, New York, were questioned by police, shown to Hyland, and released.

Two men arrested as fugitives in connection with a Pennsylvania burglary possessed a half-inch roll of Johnson & Johnson white adhesive tape, a machete, two knives, and a hatchet at the time of their arrest. Both were questioned about the Hatch murder, denied any knowledge, and passed polygraphs. A Pennsylvania man who was charged with a murder in which the victim was shot, decapitated, and had his hands cut off was fingerprinted with negative results.

The slightest irregular behavior prompted police suspicion. A couple arrested in Massachusetts and charged with public lewdness was questioned because the man had a southern accent, even though he looked nothing like the composite. A fingerprint comparison came up negative. A Massachusetts couple whose light blue sedan with temporary Colorado plates had broken down in Syracuse, causing the man to become abusive, was questioned, fingerprinted, shown to Hyland, and released. A man who was AWOL from a North Carolina Marine Corps camp and driving a blue Dodge with North Carolina plates was investigated and cleared.

There were others. Blue was a popular color for cars in the mid-1970s. Lots of people traveled in pairs. Plenty of them were in their early to mid-20s. Gas stations, especially remote ones with lone attendants, were frequent targets for crime. Unfortunately, these cases were often difficult to solve, especially if the only witness was dead.

Two other similar crimes had happened in small towns in Pennsylvania and Vermont that summer. The Pennsylvania case occurred in Phoenixville, just outside of Philadelphia. It looked a lot like the Hatch murder: A lone attendant working in an off-brand gas station was found dead in the back room, his hands and feet bound with adhesive tape, his throat slashed. A small amount of cash was missing from the register. However, the latent prints found on the adhesive tape in Pennsylvania did not match those found in New York.

The Vermont crime occurred in the town of White River Junction, along the Vermont and New Hampshire border. Again the victim was the lone attendant of a small, off-brand gas station, who had been robbed and stabbed—but this young man had also been shot. Incredibly, the victim survived and described his attacker to the police. However, the description was at odds with the composite, and the prints found didn't match the New York ones.

An unsolved gas station robbery and murder in Edmonton, Canada also occurred that same summer. But the police there had very little evidence to go on.

The breakthrough occurred on December 5, 1975. An officer in the Virginia sheriff's office who investigated the Danville murder contacted the New York authorities. The officer said that not only was Billy Ronald driving a 1970 blue Plymouth Road Runner at the time of the August 1973 Virginia killing, but his female companion, a woman named Patsy Kelly Jarrett, said that she and Billy Ronald had just come from New York State. The officer immediately sent Billy Ronald's fingerprints to New York, where they matched latent prints on a tape container at the scene of the Sherrill murder.

From that moment forward, police reports named Billy Ronald Kelly and Patsy Kelly Jarrett as the perpetrators of the Hatch murder.

A couple of weeks later, their photos were shown to Hyland.

The Virginia murder was clearly the work of Billy Ronald. It occurred at a Kayo gas station. Billy Ronald killed the attendant with a sawed-off shotgun, which Kelly never saw. A witness had seen the 1970 blue Plymouth Road Runner at the Danville station and managed to get the plate number. This led the police to Kelly, who led them to Billy Ronald. The sawed-off shotgun was found as well, bearing the same fingerprints as the adhesive tape used to bind Paul Hatch. Billy Ronald showed no remorse upon being arrested for the Virginia crime. When asked what his occupation was, he stated that he was a professional robber and killer. When New York state police later met with Billy Ronald to question him about the Hatch murder, he didn't deny it. Instead he said, "I make it a practice never to discuss anything I have been involved in with the police."

The New York police did not believe that Kelly had been an innocent bystander or unwitting accomplice in Virginia. They reasoned that the car was hers and not Billy Ronald's, she had been in it during the crime, and Billy Ronald had used a sawed-off shotgun—not the kind of thing that is easily hidden on a road trip. They were disappointed that the Virginia police had not found the Hatch murder weapon on Billy Ronald or in the car, but a knife is easily disposed of. They didn't believe that Kelly could have lived and traveled in such close quarters with Billy Ronald and not seen these weapons.

Still, the police knew they had a stronger case against Billy Ronald than Kelly. They had fingerprints, evidence of other similar conduct, and an immediate positive identification. When Kelly was arrested at around midnight on March 10, 1976, and brought to the High Point, North Carolina Police Department for questioning, she waived her rights and agreed to talk to police without an attorney present. She denied any knowledge of the murder and robbery at the Seaway station. She acknowledged that she was with Billy Ronald in New York State during July and August of 1973 and that they had lived together in Utica. She mentioned the name of a family she and Billy Ronald stayed with in Herkimer, New York, on the way to Utica. She described a "girlfriend" named Gerri, a bartender at a restaurant in Utica. She said she spent time with Gerri while Billy Ronald went his own separate way, often using her car.

But the New York police didn't believe Kelly and were determined to find holes in her story. They talked to the Herkimer family and Gerri, looking for discrepancies. They talked to people who knew Kelly and Billy Ronald in North Carolina. It's hard to know what exactly went on during those conversations. Police records reveal that much of what Kelly said was corroborated, but the police had their own spin. For example, Gerri's statement emphasized that Kelly and Billy Ronald were often together, were known as the Kellys, people assumed them to be married, and they drove a blue car. Anticipating an alibi defense, the police asked Gerri whether she might have been with Kelly on that Saturday afternoon in August. Gerri said that she was never with Kelly on a Saturday because she worked late on Friday nights and "would have to get ready to go to work the next afternoon or night at the Hub." But she also agreed that she and Kelly became "very good friends" and corresponded for at least a year after that summer.

There were other truths I can only wonder at. Paul Hatch's truth, for example. No one will ever know his truth, but it haunts me nonetheless. Did the young man know he would die when Billy Ronald bound his hands and feet and stuffed Hatch's own shirt into his mouth? When he felt himself being stabbed from behind, did he know these wounds would not threaten his life, but his throat would soon be slashed?

Reading Paul Hatch's autopsy report is unnerving. The ordinary details are the hardest. He was wearing a blue cotton work shirt with "Seaway" over the left pocket, blue jeans, and size 9 Hush Puppy shoes. He had a hand-rolled cigarette in his pants pocket. He was small, only five foot two and 140 pounds. He had thick, dark brown hair and gray eyes. He was killed 13 days before his eighteenth birthday.

The police investigation uncovered the fact that Hatch occasionally smoked marijuana but had no significant involvement in drugs. Police also learned that he had recently attended an outdoor rock concert, was an accomplished high school wrestler, and had a girlfriend.

Then there is Billy Ronald's story. I confess that, in the course of my representation of Kelly, I did not often think about Billy Ronald. I was surprisingly uncurious about him. Although this makes sense on one level—he wasn't my client and there was no need to figure out who he was or how he came to be that way—it still strikes me as odd. Perhaps I needed Billy Ronald to remain a one-dimensional villain. Sometimes it's easier when the sides are clearly drawn, and I was on Kelly's side. It could be that I simply took a page from Kelly, who rarely talked about Billy Ronald. It might also be that, although Billy Ronald was the instigating cause of Kelly's plight, he quickly became irrelevant to it. Nothing having to do with Billy Ronald was helpful to Kelly. To the contrary, most of what was uncovered about Billy Ronald—especially his other crimes—hurt her. Yet it would be useful to know more now, to know something about his life. He is an important person in the cast of characters. But my efforts have been frustrated. I contacted lawyers, court clerks, and the probation departments in both New York and Virginia, but could not obtain a copy of Billy Ronald's presentence report. I also sought information from Billy Ronald himself, but he refused. The last I heard, he was in Virginia's Powhatan Correctional Center infirmary suffering from a terminal illness. Because the court records contain only the barest biographical information, I am left to speculate.

I do not believe in the notion of a bad seed. My experience as a criminal defense lawyer has shown me that people who do terrible things usually had terrible things done to them, often early in life. As W. H. Auden once wrote, "Those to whom evil is done, Do evil in return."[37]

Perhaps evil was done to Billy Ronald. Perhaps, as an Irish friend says, complete with brogue, some people seem to have the "devil in them." Or maybe, to quote Bruce Springsteen, "There's just a meanness in the world."[38]

I have to accept that I will never know Billy Ronald's story. He remains a mystery.

~

But the truth was more complicated still for Kelly.

After Kelly was convicted and sentenced, she was sent to Albion Correctional Facility near Rochester, New York. When Albion first opened its doors in 1893 as the Western House of Refuge for Women, it was an all-female reformatory for women aged 16 to 30 who had been charged with misdemeanors or sexual waywardness. Albion went through several evolutions as a women's reformatory and then, in 1972, became a minimum-security prison for men. In 1977, however, the New York Department of Corrections created a medium-security unit for women there to relieve overcrowding at Bedford Hills. Although men and women were usually kept apart at Albion, a few activities—college courses, religious services, and the prison choir—were integrated. Kelly met the jailhouse lawyer who unsuccessfully appealed her case in the state appellate courts through Bible study.

Albion was not a very secure institution. The physical plant still looked like an old farm that had been turned into a reformatory. The fencing around the place was more symbolic than real—it might have been the same fencing once used for farm animals—and it had no barbed wire. It did not take much ingenuity for a determined inmate to make it out of Albion.

In 1979, Kelly escaped.

She ran because she was horrified at the prospect of spending her life in prison. She didn't know where to turn. The courts had failed her. The law had failed her. She doubted that a fellow inmate's efforts on her behalf would amount to anything. She was losing hope.

Yet behind her escape lay a paradoxical optimism. She believed she could break out of prison, get a job, earn enough money to hire a lawyer, and ultimately vindicate herself. Somehow, despite everything that had happened, she still believed in the justice system. If she kept trying, the truth of her innocence would come out.

Kelly managed to make her way from western New York to Manhattan's Hell's Kitchen, where she found work and a place to sleep. She then set about earning enough money to pay for a lawyer. She knew she needed the kind of advocate a rich person would hire, not an untrained jailhouse lawyer or a court-appointed one. She had tried these with no success. She washed dishes at a Midtown diner during the day and tended bar at a gay club in Greenwich Village at night. She took extra hours whenever she could. After she saved a little money, she started quietly asking coworkers whether they knew any good lawyers.

Although Kelly had told no one in the city that she was on the run or contacted family members, she had again placed her trust in someone who betrayed her. An Albion inmate looking for a way to shorten her own sentence told the authorities where they could find Kelly. Apprehended a few months later, Kelly was immediately sent to Bedford Hills.

Kelly would try to escape once more, early on in her stay there. This attempt looked less like an escape than an ill-fated tryst: After fashioning a dummy and putting it under the covers in her bunk, she got no farther than the cell of her then lover. Still, she was charged with criminal escape.

Kelly pled guilty to both escapes, and a total of three and a half years was tacked on to her 25 to life sentence. She says she pled guilty because she *was* guilty. She had no trouble taking her punishment, despite the fact that the attempted escapes were the product of her wrongful imprisonment. She would take responsibility for what she had done but not for what she had not.

Kelly's time in prison was significantly affected by the escape convictions. Her chances of getting out—by clemency or parole—were also harmed. In the prison system, few things are worse than an escape risk. Once Kelly was known to be one, Bedford Hills designated her a "tracker." This is a label for inmates who need to be under close surveillance. Kelly was not allowed to go anywhere in the prison without being searched—often a full-body strip search—and without her whereabouts being duly noted by authorities. Certain prison jobs were off limits to her. The possibility of living on the Honors Floor, the almost-certain destination of most long-term prisoners for good behavior, was not something that Kelly could look forward to.

Almost from the start, Kelly was doing hard time in prison, the hardest kind of time. Not only was she under constant watch, but she was housed not with her peers—women who were doing 10 and 20 years, who had accepted Bedford Hills as their home and had earned certain privileges—but with younger and often more violent prisoners. Also, due to the closure of several public psychiatric hospitals, more and more mentally ill women were being incarcerated. Because of the shortage of space and lack of resources, many times they were housed with the general prison population. Kelly was often unable to sleep because of the ranting of mentally ill prisoners in her cellblock.

Sometimes Kelly thought she was going crazy too. She couldn't make sense of her life. How had she ended up behind bars in New York, a place where she had spent a few pleasant weeks one summer? How could she have been found guilty of a crime she knew nothing about? How could she be serving a life sentence?

But Kelly at least had her truth: She was innocent. Not only did this essential truth shape every decision she made, it also shaped the way she regarded, and ultimately coped with, her incarceration. The years in prison were bearable only because she did not dishonor herself by lying. In serving her sentence she was also serving the truth.

Kelly placed her faith in the truth, and truth became a kind of faith for her. It was a fundamentalist faith.

For Kelly, the truth of her innocence could not be adjusted or modified for the sake of expediency, nor could it give way to other values. Truth was everything because it was all she had.

It is no wonder that Kelly could not meaningfully consider the robbery plea she was offered before her trial in March 1977 or the time-served plea that was offered after she won her habeas petition in March 1986. Each plea offer required Kelly to lie and say she was involved in the murder of Paul Hatch. With each plea rejection, her commitment to the truth—and her belief in it— became more fierce.

It is no wonder that, looking back, Kelly maintains that she did the right thing in rejecting those pleas—even during the 19 long years that followed her rejection of the plea that would have resulted in her freedom. She was true to herself.

Chapter 3

Hope

When I was a law student, my visits with Kelly were unstructured and informal. Although they were "legal visits"—I signed the official prison visitor book, handed over my ID for the duration of the visit, and we sometimes met in the one of the "official" visiting rooms off the main room—they were not like the lawyer-client interviews I read about in the clinic seminar.[1] I don't think I ever had a by-the-book lawyer-client interview with Kelly. It was always more like a conversation.

No doubt I wanted to be "lawyerly" and "professional" with her, but the exact shape of the role I was playing was still a mystery to me. I was only just learning how to be a lawyer. I was a novice, a rookie. I had worked with lawyers and clients before. During college I had been a student intern at two different public interest law offices in New Haven, after college I had been a VISTA (Volunteer in Service to America—known as the domestic Peace Corps) at the local legal aid office, and I had spent the summer after my first year of law school working in the criminal unit of the same legal aid office. But this was different. In many ways Kelly was my first client as an actual almost lawyer. And the truth was, I didn't know what the hell I was doing.

Of course, this is why I was in the clinic: to learn about being a lawyer by *doing* it (under supervision and as part of a program of study that included plenty of reading, discussion, and "structured reflection"). But I didn't want to be a sorry excuse for a lawyer, learning at the client's expense. Even though Claudia was an excellent supervisor, I didn't want to turn to her constantly. So I did my best to try to figure out my own lawyering style: how to present myself, how to integrate my "real self" into my lawyer self, and how to go about negotiating appropriate professional boundaries. I had some good models—lawyers I had liked and admired over the years—and now I had Claudia. But I wanted to find the right fit for me.

I was tested by Kelly early on. Although she didn't ask me to touch an intimate body part—that was, thankfully, a one-time experience—she did get unexpectedly personal the second time I met with her. She asked me whether I was gay.

Again, I looked around for Claudia, who was nowhere to be found. I thought of seeking the advice of another law student who had gone to the prison with me, a friend who was meeting with another client. But this seemed odd. First, I would have to say to Kelly, "Excuse me a moment while I consult with my friend about this question." Second, I didn't think my friend possessed any greater wisdom about what to do in this situation than I did. So I punted. I said, "Why do you ask?" Kelly said that she just had a feeling, there was something about me that made her feel comfortable. She assured me that if I wasn't gay, that was fine too.

I told her she had good intuition.

The truth is, my sexuality has always been a bit complicated, or at least not terribly *fixed,* and this was especially so in law school. While it wasn't a secret that I had had relationships with women as well as men, I didn't go around broadcasting my sexual orientation. I wasn't sure exactly what I should say to Kelly, what word or words to use to describe how I saw myself. When Kelly asked me that question, I had had more girlfriends than boyfriends, yet this was more a reflection of how discerning I was about men than it was a sign of my "true orientation." (My standards were so high that two of my boyfriends would later receive MacArthur "Genius" awards.) During the time I worked with Kelly in law school, I had one somewhat serious relationship with a man, a crush on another (a good friend who, alas, had a longtime girlfriend), and several relationships with women, of varying degrees of seriousness.

Poor Kelly! She had no idea what her question stirred up. But she wasn't looking for a lengthy dissertation on the complexity of my sex life. She just wanted to know if we had this one thing in common.

So I made this disclosure. We made that connection.

There has been only one other time when a client broached the topic of my sexual orientation. Shortly after I joined the Philadelphia public defender's office, I was assigned to a day of "office interviewing." At the bail hearing, clients were instructed to come to the office right away if they got out. Interviewing lawyers saw them on a first-come, first-serve basis.

It was a Monday, and the waiting room was packed. I was wearing a skirt, blouse, and low-heeled pumps. After conducting a couple of interviews, I picked up the next file and called out the client's name. A tall, broad-shouldered African American woman came forward. She took one look at me and said loudly—she might as well have used a bullhorn: "What? Just because I get arrested near a gay bar I get *you* for a lawyer?"

Feeling my face grow hot, I ushered the client into a private interviewing room. After she sat down, she leaned across the table for closer scrutiny and remarked, "You're Jewish too, aren't you?" I said, "Look, I appreciate your interest, but do you think maybe we could talk about you and your case?"

It turned out she had a fairly substantial history of mental illness. Sometimes the mentally ill can be pretty sharp. They see things the rest of us miss.

Many years after meeting Kelly, after I became involved with my partner, Sally, and we were raising our son, Joe, people would occasionally ask whether my devotion to Kelly had to do with our shared sexual orientation. I have never known how to answer this question. Motivations are often multifaceted. I know that I was moved by Kelly and her plight from the very beginning, and being gay was a big part of Kelly's identity. She liked saying she was "gay and proud" and often wrote that slogan in her letters. But I believe I would have been moved by Kelly whether she was gay or straight. It was her innocence, not her sexual orientation, that made me want to get her out of prison.

But maybe my dismissal of the gay question is too glib. I am interested in what motivates people and understand why others would be curious about it. So I have tried to think harder about the question. Might similarity or familiarity be motivators for me? Might I have seen myself in Kelly and, for this reason, been prompted to act for her? I still think not. While I felt a connection with Kelly—because we were close in age, because she was a woman, because she was gay, because she needed help, because I liked her—as in other relationships, *sameness* was not the overriding factor. Kelly and I have always been more different than alike. She is a southern, small-town, working-class, high school–educated, deeply religious Catholic. I am a northern, big-city (though raised in the suburbs), educated, Jewish professional. Where Kelly is devout, attends mass daily, and believes in the power of prayer, I am secular and skeptical. I often say that as a Reform Jew, I observe the High Holidays, Passover, and the Academy Awards. (I admit that I stole this from a rabbinical stand-up comedy competition.) Where Kelly is gay and proud, my sexual orientation has never been my primary identity, and I tend to resist clubs and labels. Other things come first: my ethnicity, my professional identity, my left-feminist worldview, my sense of humor.

Moreover, my work as a criminal defense lawyer does not usually involve representing people with whom I have much in common. Generally speaking, I represent impoverished, undereducated, nonwhite men who commit urban street crime. Kelly—an innocent, white country girl—is an anomaly.

Next to Kelly, my longest lawyer-client relationship was with a damaged—terribly abused and neglected—black youth who was facing the prospect of adult trial on two counts of armed rape. The crimes were ugly. There was no question he had committed them. I took his case because he was in trouble and needed representation. This client and I had basically nothing in common. Indeed, I had more in common with his alleged victims than I did with him: one was a recent college graduate doing inner-city public service work who was so traumatized by what happened that she quit her job and joined the Peace Corps in Africa. Still, I had no trouble representing this young man—there was more to him than his crimes—and I became fond of him, notwithstanding our "differences."

In more than 25 years of law practice, the client with whom I probably had most in common was a woman named Claudia Brenner. Brenner was not a criminal defendant. She was the victim of a shooting on the Appalachian Trail in Pennsylvania in 1988, in which her female partner, Rebecca Wight, was killed. The shooter, Stephen Roy Carr, was a "mountain man" who had come upon Brenner and Wight on the trail and followed them as they hiked in a remote area. He shot them with a single-gauge shotgun after watching them have sex. Brenner was hit five times—four times in the face and neck—but managed to hike several miles in the dark and flag down a car. Wight bled to death from a single bullet that struck her kidney.

Carr confessed to the crime when he was arrested. But he later tried to claim he was provoked by the sight of two women making love, putting forward what some call the "homosexual panic" defense.[2]

I got involved in the case at the urging of a friend of Brenner's who contacted me shortly after she was rushed to a hospital, and then at Brenner's own request. She wanted a feminist lawyer who would represent her interests. Victim representation was relatively new and undefined at the time, and I had never represented anyone other than criminal defendants. But Brenner persuaded me that I might be of service.

Brenner and I were different in many ways: She was an avid hiker and I am not; she, like Kelly, was strongly lesbian-identified and I am not; and she and her "lesbian family" were into a kind of spiritualism that, frankly, I can't bear. However, we also had some things in common. We were both Jewish, Ivy League–educated feminists in our early 30s. We had a similar smart-alecky sense of humor. We had the same Patagonia jacket.

Still, although my allegiance was solidly with Brenner, during the court proceedings I couldn't help but be curious about, and curiously drawn to, her assailant. The 28-year-old Carr was not appealing physically: He was pale, scrawny, hunched over, acne scarred, and in need of a hair wash. His crime was appalling: He had stalked and gunned down two women who had done absolutely nothing to him and had succeeded in murdering one. Yet he also struck me as pathetic, as if he'd been kicked around his whole life. Notwithstanding his evil act, Carr seemed more screwed up than evil. Despite the fact that he had the telltale three names of a killer—like Lee Harvey Oswald, James Earl Ray, and John Wilkes Booth—this was Carr's first-ever violent crime. He was a naïf compared to Billy Ronald. The defense lawyer in me wanted to know more about him. The defense lawyer in me felt for him, because he was facing capital charges. I wondered what I would do if I had been appointed to represent him.

When, relying on an argument I had developed, the judge prohibited Carr from offering a provocation defense, he pled guilty to murder and received a sentence of life without the possibility of parole. Brenner preferred this to obtaining a death sentence, and apparently so did the defendant. I did too.

There have been plenty of other clients with whom I shared things in common. One of my favorites was an African American medical student accused of assaulting two white police officers in a "driving while black" case. The young black man was in a late-model car when he allegedly ran a stop sign in a residential neighborhood. When he protested, the officers dragged him out of the car, threw him to the ground, and handcuffed him.

The case went to trial and was hard fought. The police maintained that my client was the aggressor. We argued that whatever actions he had taken were minimal (the officers were uninjured) and in self-defense (he only tried to ward off *their* attack). My client had never been in trouble and was in all regards exemplary: good student, good citizen, good person. After several hours of deliberation, an all-white jury acquitted. For some years after the trial, the client would call me on his birthday and thank me for what I had done. This sort of thing doesn't happen very often. Most clients would just as soon forget about the circumstances under which we met. Few keep in touch.

The only criminal defendant I ever represented who was a white Jewish woman was someone I'll call Mindi, who used to sign her name with a smiley face above the *i* instead of a dot. She was accused of failing to deposit $10,000 in cash receipts from the health food store she managed. When confronted by the police, she denied any wrongdoing but said she'd pay back the money in installments.

Mindi told me that she had made that statement to the police because she was scared of going to jail and not because she actually took the money. She wanted to go to trial. She showed up at my office and every court date in a fur coat and expensive-looking jewelry. I explained to her that she would have to dress more modestly at trial unless she wanted the jury to think that she committed the crime to support her extravagant lifestyle. She was aghast. "This isn't even real fur," she said.

Somehow I managed to persuade her. She appeared for jury selection in a perfect blue dress with a string of pearls. I was pleased.

She took me aside and said she needed a favor. "I want you to promise me something," she said. I had never seen her so anxious. "Sure, what?" I asked. "No matter what happens at trial, no matter what the verdict is, and no matter what the sentence is, never tell anyone you saw me in this dress," she said.

Of all the criminal defendants I represented over the years, Kelly has always been special. From the very start, I did unusual things for her. During the summer of my second year in law school, I organized a softball game between the Bedford Hills team and my own team, the New Haven Feminist Union. It took a lot of arranging to play a team that obviously never traveled. All of my teammates needed a security clearance months in advance before they would be allowed on prison grounds.

The game was memorable, less for the play than for the atmosphere. Every visiting player who came up to bat was heckled. Anyone who made a poor fielding play was called Butter Fingers. Anyone with a distinctive physical feature had this pointed out: Our pitcher was called Needle-nose; our first baseman Chicken Legs.

Swinging for the fence had a whole new meaning when the fence was topped with barbed wire.

Kelly played second base and I played shortstop. I think we each got a couple of hits.

⌒

It is hard to generalize about what motivates lawyers to represent the criminally accused, especially in seemingly hopeless cases. There are undoubtedly as many motivations as there are defenders. Still, some ties bind most of us.

In what I consider the best law review article on the subject, "Defending the Guilty," Professor Barbara Babcock offers five different reasons for defending alleged criminals:

1. The "garbage collector's reason" (it's dirty work but someone has to do it, the adversary system requires lawyers on both sides)
2. The "legalistic or positivist reason" (truth cannot be known, guilt is a legal conclusion)
3. The "political activist's reason" (most of those who commit crime have themselves suffered injustice and oppression)
4. The "humanitarian" or "social worker's reason" (most criminals are disadvantaged and ought to be treated with humanity and respect)
5. The "egotist's reason" (defense work is more interesting, challenging, and rewarding than the work done by most lawyers)[3]

In the same article, Babcock shares a story about a client she once represented—a pitiful woman she called "Geraldine" who was facing a long sentence for a minor drug offense because of her record. Feeling strongly that her client should not go to prison, Babcock fashioned a defense and went to trial. While Geraldine sat through the trial impassively, appearing unconcerned about her fate, Babcock did battle, nearly coming to blows with the prosecutor. When the jury came back with a verdict of not guilty by reason of insanity, Geraldine suddenly jumped up and threw her arms around Babcock, declaring "I'm so happy for you."[4]

Sometimes we are more motivated than our clients.

Reflecting on her own time as a public defender, Babcock concludes that defenders have a "peculiar mind-set, heart-set, soul-set."[5] Either you have the chops for the work or you don't.

I agree that there is such a thing as a "natural" defender. A former colleague was instantly recognized as a defender in law school. He had enrolled in the criminal defense clinic in preparation for becoming a prosecutor, which he believed would be his life's work. After a few weeks, his teachers sat him down. "Bookman," they said (using his last name, as most people do). "We need to tell you something and you may not like it. We've been watching you. You're a defender, not a prosecutor. It's in your blood." And they were right. More than 25 years later, he's still at it.

Still, some cases test even those with a defender mind-set, heart-set, and soul-set. These cases tend to involve either the truly innocent or truly guilty. Kelly is an example of the former: Her decades-long incarceration was a constant blow to all of her lawyers. Any number of odious crimes could serve as examples of the latter. The appalling and sometimes horrifying behavior of some clients can test the will of the most committed lawyer.

But sometimes lawyers get it wrong and assume bad behavior when there might not be any. For example, a Virginia lawyer who was perfectly willing to accept a routine immigration fraud case soon after September 11 became visibly distressed and sought to withdraw when the government claimed the case was connected to the World Trade Center attacks.[6] He did so even though his client vigorously denied being a terrorist and said all he had done was allow a friend to use his address to obtain a driver's license. Like many swept up by law enforcement following September 11, the client—an Indonesian national and Muslim—was presumed guilty, even by his own attorney.[7]

I believe that the lawyers who agreed to defend these post-September 11 cases were heroes. By ensuring that those accused of the very worst crimes had the same basic rights as those accused of more ordinary offenses, these lawyers were not only protecting their client; they were protecting all of us. The criminal lawyer's role is bigger than any one case. As Supreme Court Justice William Brennan once said, criminal lawyers uphold the "charter of human rights, dignity, and self-determination" embodied in the American Bill of Rights.[8] These rights include the right to due process of law, trial by jury, and confrontation of witnesses as well as the right to be free from unlawful searches and seizures, compelled self-incrimination, and cruel and unusual punishment. Indeed, criminal lawyers are the embodiment of the most important of all rights, the right to counsel, which is inextricably connected to the ability to assert all other rights.

Another commentator, Harvard law professor Charles Ogletree, has a different view of what motivates defenders. Reflecting on his own days as a public defender, Professor Ogletree argues that "empathy" and "heroism" are the motivations that sustain public defenders and criminal lawyers.[9] To Ogletree, the best and most enduring defenders are those who are able to build close, caring, empathic relationships with clients, relationships that approximate a "true friendship,"[10] and who, like latter-day Robin Hoods, are willing to engage in heroic battle against enormous odds to save the oppressed and underdog.[11]

Although Ogletree's notions of empathy and heroism resonate with many defenders, I have never felt comfortable with this model. I worry that the sort of empathy Ogletree endorses leads to porous professional boundaries, an idealized view of the lawyer-client relationship, and a feeling of constant devastation when things don't work out for the client. I once tried to convey this last concern to a young lawyer under my supervision. She was disconsolate about a client with an indefensible case and a lengthy record who had just received a relatively short prison sentence. She pronounced the case "tragic." I suggested that it might be wiser to think of it as "unfortunate" rather than tragic—just to pace herself.

As for Ogletree's heroism—which is defined largely as *winning cases*—I worry that defenders don't win often enough to feel heroic. When we do win, many of our clients get in trouble again so the victory can feel short-lived. I am concerned as well about the grandiosity of wanting to be a hero, and the built-in paternalism. Most defenders are white and middle class. Who elected us the saviors of the poor, black masses? Not everyone looks good in Robin Hood's tights.

My own motivations are a mix of the political activist, the social worker, the egotist, and the civil libertarian. I tell students and young lawyers that I would rather have them respect clients than befriend them, and the best way to convey respect is by diligent preparation, careful counseling, and zealous advocacy. I want them to be excellent lawyers, working to develop and perfect their professional craft, not heroes. I often have to remind them that winning is not the only measure of good lawyering.

I also do my best to instill in students a "sense of outrage," a phrase I borrowed from my friend Ilene, a fellow clinical teacher and poverty lawyer. She tells her students, "If you're not outraged, you're not paying attention." What she means is you don't have to spend much time in criminal, housing, or family court to witness the routine abuse of power, randomness of justice, and ravages of poverty and inequality. Most poor people's lawyers have a deep and pervasive sense of outrage.[12]

I believe that for motivations to be truly sustaining, they must offer a combination of altruism, egoism, and activism. For defenders, the altruistic piece is serving the client with respect, devotion, and zeal. The egoistic piece is the satisfaction we derive from developing our craft. The activist piece is making a difference client by client when we channel outrage into advocacy.

But even highly motivated lawyers hit the wall now and then. Sometimes there's no productive outlet for outrage. Sometimes it all just seems so hopeless.

To the uninitiated, a lawyer putting body and soul into a losing case like Kelly's is a curious, even wrongheaded thing. Kelly had already lost repeatedly, at trial and in three of four appeals. The road ahead was bleak. Why persist? Especially when resources are scarce—and there are plenty of prisoners in dire need of counsel— why not wait for a case where a lawyer might actually make a difference? Why not cut my losses and move on?

It is hard to explain some attachments. From when I first got to know Kelly as a law student, and through my years as an increasingly experienced lawyer, I had always seen Kelly as a compelling figure. She was a living embodiment of the fallibility of the criminal justice system. Hers was the very tragedy I was devoting my professional life to preventing. But she wasn't just any wrongfully convicted person; I had come to know her. I met her when she was still very much a girl, still full of hope. I saw how the years had changed her. She wasn't just any tragic figure; she was *my* tragic figure. While Kelly languished in prison, a piece of me was there too.

As the years of Kelly's incarceration passed—after I graduated from law school, after Kelly turned down that last plea offer—I went from being a public defender to a law teacher to a combination of the two: a clinical law teacher running a criminal defense clinic. I lived in Philadelphia, New York, Philadelphia again, and then Boston. I took a job at Harvard Law School, helping to create and direct a criminal justice program that provided representation for the indigent accused and conducted research on a range of criminal justice issues.

Life was busy. I had plenty of clients, plenty of students, plenty of projects. I thought of Kelly from time to time, but it was painful to do so. She had won and she had lost. Her victory in the federal district court had been incredibly short-lived. The reversal in the federal appeals court stood.

I felt comforted by the fact that Kelly had been represented by excellent lawyers. Aside from Claudia, at least two other NYU law professors had contributed to her habeas petition, Anthony Amsterdam and Randy Hertz. Amsterdam is a latter-day Clarence Darrow. He literally wrote the book on criminal defense advocacy[13] and is a renowned death penalty litigator, having argued the case that overturned the U.S. death penalty in 1973, *Furman v. Georgia.* Hertz was a respected trial attorney at the Public Defender Service of the District of Columbia before becoming a clinical law teacher specializing in juvenile justice.

Whatever was happening with her case, I figured Kelly was in good hands. She certainly didn't need me.

Then, in 1993, in the course of representing a Massachusetts woman who had killed her abusive husband—my efforts were part of a state-wide campaign to obtain clemency (pardon or commutation) for a handful of women serving time for killing abusive partners—I helped organize a conference on women in prison at Harvard Law School. The keynote speaker was Jean Harris, who had recently been released from Bedford Hills Prison after serving 12 years.

I felt that I knew Jean Harris. Not only had her case been highly publicized, but I had seen her in the Bedford Hills visiting room many times when I visited Kelly. She was easy to spot. The dignified, middle-aged former private school headmistress had the uncanny ability to make the required Bedford Hills prisoner uniform, which consisted of at least one dark green item, look like a private school uniform. She somehow looked classy in her dark green cardigan sweater with a white blouse underneath, complete with a collar pin, and sometimes a matching green skirt. She often carried a clipboard, as if she were organizing a social.

When I introduced myself to Harris, I said she probably wouldn't remember me, but I used to spend a lot of time at Bedford Hills visiting Patsy Kelly Jarrett. She reacted immediately. "Oh, Kelly," she said. "Everyone knows she's innocent."

Harris mentioned that she had written about Kelly in one of her books.[14] She could have written about any number of women—many at Bedford Hills had compelling stories—but Kelly stood out. Not only did Harris believe that Kelly was innocent of any crime, she found her utterly innocent in every way. She recalled being struck by Kelly's goodness when they first met in prison.[15] She had not forgotten her.

Harris told me that Kelly had been working as a nurse's aide in the prison infirmary taking care of women with AIDS and cancer and that this had become a vocation for her. Kelly volunteered to work with prisoners with AIDS, Harris said, when no one knew how the disease was contracted and when many corrections staff were afraid to touch these women. Kelly was said to attend to those in her care with extraordinary kindness, a rare enough quality in prison under ordinary circumstances. Harris did not disguise her admiration for Kelly.

Harris said she didn't know the current status of Kelly's case, but urged me to contact her.

I wrote to Kelly. I apologized for being out of touch, told her what I'd been doing since we had last corresponded, and recounted the conversation with Jean Harris. I asked about her health, her family, and her case. I wondered whether a clemency petition had ever been filed on her behalf and what she thought about this idea. She wrote back and said that a friend—a former prisoner who, like Harris, believed in her innocence—and the friend's husband were putting together a clemency petition. Neither was a lawyer, but they wanted to help. Kelly said she didn't think the petition would amount to anything, but she was glad that her friend had not forgotten her. She was happy to hear from me.

I asked whether she would like me to write a letter in support of clemency for the petition. Maybe I could find a lawyer in New York to assist her friends in drafting the petition? Maybe I could find a lawyer in New York to provide whatever legal assistance she might need?

Although I was licensed to practice law in New York, I didn't offer myself. I had just spent months pursuing clemency for a prisoner in my own state, an effort that had involved many trips to the prison (to work with the client, meet with prison employees, and collect prison records) and many trips to the far-off town where the crime occurred (to talk to witnesses, jurors, and the client's family, and to visit the crime scene). It helps to be local.

Maybe I didn't offer myself because I needed the distance. There was something about Kelly's case that threatened my usual equilibrium. It was Kelly herself—her familiarity, her vulnerability, the fact that I had known her since I was a kid myself—and also the enormity of her innocence. I was no longer a law student working for someone else who bore ultimate responsibility. Her innocence would be on my shoulders. There had to be someone better.

I told Kelly I would find her a lawyer I trusted, a good lawyer and a good person. Then I set about finding one. I was surprised by how difficult it was. I had quite a few friends in New York who were criminal lawyers, but for one reason or another—an already onerous workload, other life demands, and perhaps also recognition of how emotionally draining the undertaking would be—no one was eager to take the case.

One friend finally agreed to do it. I'll call her "Susan." Susan was a prisoners rights lawyer at a New York legal aid office who used to be a colleague of mine at the Philadelphia public defender's. I thought it was a good match: She was a very good lawyer, and Kelly's case would fit right in to her caseload. I also thought Susan and Kelly would like each other and work well together. I emphasized to Susan how important Kelly was to me and said she shouldn't agree to do it unless she would throw herself into it. I knew it was a lot to ask, but I needed her to be nothing less than a stand-in for me. Still, I told Susan, her friendship with *me* would not be enough to see her through—it was *Kelly* who needed her friendship.

Susan said she understood and would do it. But she never did. She didn't go to the prison to meet Kelly. She didn't do the minimal things lawyers do to establish rapport and trust with clients (especially one who had been represented by a constantly changing army of students). Instead, she wrote Kelly a couple of lawyerly letters with requests for information and instructions to call her at her office. When I tried to question Susan gently about her efforts, she reacted defensively and blamed Kelly. When things didn't change after a couple of months, I told Kelly she should tell Susan she was fired.

My friendship with Susan never recovered.

After this, it didn't feel right to entrust Kelly to anyone else. I realized I had to do it myself. I should have known this from the start. If I felt so strongly about Kelly, how could I not do it? The distance between Cambridge and New York would make things difficult, but if Kelly was willing to accept that we wouldn't be able to meet as often as we might like, I would do all I could to make it work. I was fortunate to have the resources of Harvard Law School—smart students, plenty of research tools, and financial support—and New York was not *that* far way. Kelly was pleased.

A number of questions—personal, professional, philosophical, psychological—are raised when a lawyer undertakes a righteous but hopeless case. I was vaguely aware of some of these questions when I made the decision to represent Kelly again, but as the years went by, old questions resurfaced and new questions cropped up. Answers were few and fleeting.

The most difficult of the questions has to do with hope itself. The act of providing hope where there is little can plague a lawyer as well as a client. When a lawyer takes on a cause—out of belief in the cause, belief in the client, professional obligation, or ego gratification—hopes inevitably are raised. But the client bears the brunt of these raised hopes.

The more we worked on Kelly's case, the more hopeful she became, even as she and I both tried to temper those hopes. Her attitude became clear in her letters to me. Soon after my reappearance in her case, Kelly wrote: "Abbe, I hope to win my life back through you, but even if I must remain here I will never forget your care and concern about my life." Some months later she wrote: "When I hear from you I remember that you care about my life. Each time I receive a letter I have hope that one day—someday—I can be free."

I understood that, for Kelly, I was like a knight in shining armor. A former student who had worked on her case had come back as an experienced criminal lawyer now teaching at Harvard, of all places. Kelly was so grateful that I hadn't forgotten her. So many others had come and gone. There seemed to be a curious power in my return, a coming full circle, a sign of something big to come. Maybe now at last she would be vindicated.

But this was a potential problem for both of us. The drama of my return fed both of our hopes and fantasies. Kelly's greatest hope had always been that she would one day be free. But in 1986, when the federal appeals court ruled against her, reinstating her conviction, Kelly largely put away that hope and did her best to fend off that fantasy. She had been biding her time with no legal challenge to her imprisonment, no outlet for hope, for seven years when I reentered her life. She hadn't been able to hope about her future in the face of cold reality. What good would it have done? What good would it do now?

I had my own fantasies. Though I have said that I don't like the lawyer-as-hero model, I understand its appeal, especially with an innocent client. You can't help but want to rescue that client.

The more you like the client, the stronger the urge to rescue. The problem is the accompanying grandiosity, if not megalomania— the sense of oneself as all-powerful. I alone could right a long-standing wrong that no one else has managed to budge. Could I be that powerful?

The thought that I might be able to save Kelly when everyone else had failed was seductive, but I knew I had to resist the fantasy. Such fantasies can cause lawyers to say things they will regret, promise things they can't always deliver. One of the most talented lawyers I know fell into this trap. She was representing a battered woman on trial for killing her husband, and very much believed in her client. Though she had never done so before, in a heated moment she said to the client, "I promise I'll get you out of this." When the client was convicted and sentenced to 15 to life, the lawyer could not get her own words out of her head. She felt that not only did she lose a case she should have won, but she betrayed the client. The first thing is hard enough for a lawyer to endure; the second is unbearable.

I have been tempted to say the same thing to clients from time to time. I certainly *want* to get some clients out of their situations. Whenever I am overcome by the injustice of a client's prosecution, conviction, or sentence, and the words *I'll get you out of this* come to mind, I quickly channel them into other, more appropriate words. I say, "I'll fight for you," or "I'll do everything in my power on your behalf." The fear with Kelly was that out of belief in her, belief in me, and something that came awfully close to love, I would say *I will get you out of this, Kelly.*

Thank God I never did.

But what to do with those feelings? And what about all that talk of respect, of clear professional boundaries, of pacing oneself?

Who was I kidding? I could talk the talk, but when it came down to following my own creed, I was failing miserably. I was awash in my own need to succeed.

I worried about what I was offering Kelly this time around. Was I offering to start from scratch with her case and go wherever it took me? Was I just signing on to draft a clemency petition? Wouldn't all of this raise Kelly's hopes—most of which centered on the unlikeliest of prospects, obtaining a new trial and being exonerated by the United States Supreme Court? How could I raise her hopes *again* only to have them dashed? I was afraid of getting her hopes up and how much work her case would entail.

I was unsure how to manage the question of hope with Kelly. I didn't know whether hope was a good thing for her—something that would sustain her through her years of incarceration and perhaps the rest of her life—or a bad thing—a foolish fantasy that would render her incapable of coping with the reality of her circumstances. One of my favorite exchanges in the great prison movie *Shawshank Redemption* tries to get at this. Red, a lifer played by Morgan Freeman, says to the newly imprisoned Andy, played by Tim Robbins: "Hope is a dangerous thing. Hope can drive a man insane." Andy disagrees. "[T]here are places in the world that aren't made of stone," he says. "[T]here's something inside . . . that they can't get to, that they can't touch." When Red asks him what he's talking about, Andy answers, "Hope."[16]

Criminal lawyer and writer Joe Margulies calls hope "the most precious commodity in any prisoner's life."[17] Although this sounds right to me, I worry about my professional duty to be honest with clients. There have been times when the hope/honesty dilemma has felt especially acute and I feared I was striking the wrong balance. I have consulted several mental health professionals about this question. I wanted to know whether people could live without hope, and whether it was a good or bad idea to rouse hope in a hopeless case. They all shared Andy's and Margulies's view: Hope is intrinsically a good thing; people need something to believe in; a slim hope is better than no hope at all. But I still had doubts. They didn't know Kelly. If she was going to spend the rest of her life in prison, I might not be doing her any favors by stirring up hope.

So, I made a special effort to be clear and forthright with her. I told her that although there was nothing I wanted more than her freedom, we both had to be sober about our chances. No matter how hard I worked, or how much I cared, this effort was a long shot. I was willing to explore every option for her, including filing a further appeal, getting the police and prosecution to reopen the case, and pursuing clemency. But I believed that executive clemency provided her only real chance of release, and this was un-likely in her case.[18] If only she had been a battered woman, a one-time drug peddler, an elderly prisoner with a heart condition, or, best of all, someone with political connections. These prisoners are much better prospects for clemency.

Kelly was not surprised. She did not think that she had a chance of being granted clemency. Moreover, she didn't even want clemency; she wanted *vindication*. As she wrote in 1996, "In my heart I know that I must return to court and get a fair trial. I must prove my innocence. Clemency is mostly given to people in for drugs. . . . I really want to go back into court and *win* my case, Abbe. The clemency is not hopeful for me."

Kelly and I were both right about clemency being unlikely. When I got reinvolved in her case, Mario Cuomo was governor of New York. Although he was opposed to the death penalty and was in many respects an old-fashioned liberal, Cuomo was stingy when it came to granting clemency. One news reporter remarked that, under Governor Mario Cuomo, grants of clemency were "almost as rare as prison breakouts."[19] For example, notwithstanding Jean Harris's exemplary behavior in prison and widespread public support—the prison superintendent, trial judge, and jury foreperson all favored her release—it took 12 years, three clemency petitions, three books, advancing age, and imminent coronary bypass surgery before Cuomo granted her clemency.[20]

The word about Cuomo was that, because of his opposition to the death penalty, he could not afford to appear soft on crime. That's why he did not commute prison sentences. But Cuomo was hardly soft on crime. During his administration, the number of New York prison cells more than doubled, average prison sentences for violent felony offenses climbed from 38.2 months to 45.2 months, and thousands of new police officers were put on the streets. Meanwhile, the number of executive pardons and clemencies dropped from 155 granted during previous Governor Hugh Carey's eight years in office to only 31 during the 12 years under Cuomo.[21]

I told Kelly that things looked grim not only because of the serious nature of her conviction but because she had absolutely no constituency or clout. In addition to not being an abused woman, a drug mule, a former antiwar activist, or the headmistress of a fancy private school, she was not even from New York. I was willing to reach out to potential constituencies, such as the gay or Catholic communities, but I doubted that I would be able to galvanize either one.

The gay community posed a particular challenge. Although Kelly identified as a lesbian and concern about antigay bias had influenced trial strategy, the case was hard to characterize as a gay rights case. Also, the gay community has traditionally been allied more with those urging victims' rights than defendants' rights. What Kelly needed was an organization devoted to lesbians wrongly convicted of murder. If such an organization existed, it was a well-kept secret.

The Catholic community held more promise because of Kelly's longstanding support from the Bedford Hills clergy and because the church has political clout. Cuomo was Catholic, as was his successor, George Pataki. Still, I wasn't sure how I was going to get access to powerful Catholics.

I told Kelly the problem with her case was that she was *just plain innocent,* and nobody cares about the wrongful conviction of innocent people unless it's happening to them or someone they know.

In some ways, wrongly convicted prisoners serving life sentences are worse off than those facing death. The lifers receive far less public attention and less attention from the organized bar. Although this is understandable—death cases are arguably more urgent, more fraught, more *final*—I often wonder how many unknown Kellys are fading away in prisons across the country.

Wilbert Rideau, a rare famous lifer (his death sentence for a 1961 bank robbery and murder was overturned after *Furman v. Georgia*) and an award-winning writer and editor (he was editor in chief of the prison magazine *The Angolite*), wrote a haunting essay about the lonely, anonymous deaths of lifers at the Louisiana State Penitentiary, prisoners who were abandoned long ago by the outside world. These men are buried in cheap beige coffins made of a synthetic material that bears a faint resemblance to wood. The word "HEAD" is written across one end with a Magic Marker so people know which end is which.[22]

Like Kelly, Rideau got out of prison in 2005. Over the years, Rideau, an African American, had succeeded in challenging his conviction several times only to be convicted again by successive all-white juries. His fourth jury—a racially mixed one—found him guilty of manslaughter only. He had served 44 years, many more than the maximum for manslaughter.

When I offered my services to Kelly, I knew that I was raising her hopes no matter how careful I was. Listing the things I planned to do on her behalf raised hope. Scheduling a prison visit raised hope. Getting a new crop of students involved raised hope.

I wasn't at all sure this was a good thing.

After recruiting a couple of students, I set out to do what I could. First I got the files, trial transcript, and police reports for Kelly's case from New York University, and the students and I pored through them. There was a strange symmetry to this for me. I was poring through Kelly's papers again, only this time I was a clinical teacher supervising my own students.

The files included press clippings about Kelly's arrest and trial, some of which were new to me. One clipping included a photograph of Billy Ronald being taken into custody in shackles a few months before the trial. He looked intense and handsome, more handsome than I remembered. Bearded, and with a full head of dark hair pulled back in a ponytail, he looked like a cross between a young James Taylor and Dennis Hopper, with a hint of Charles Manson (but maybe this was because of the prison jumpsuit and shackles). The files also included notes about the habeas proceedings, notes about the rejected plea offer, and Billy Ronald's affidavit.

The students and I brainstormed about unanswered questions in Kelly's case and how we might go about getting answers. Then we drove to Bedford Hills.

It was good to see Kelly again after all those years. Good to see her face, to hug her, to be in her presence. But it was also sad. Sad to find Kelly older, grayer, and heavier. When Kelly was first incarcerated she weighed just over 100 pounds. Now she was closer to 200. She was also not so lighthearted anymore. I understood why her heart might be heavy these 10 years later. Mine was heavy too. In the years we'd been apart so much had happened in my life. So little had happened in hers.

I realize that I might have an unfairly narrow view of Kelly's time in prison. Who am I to say that her life there was less full than the lives many people lead? Do my worldly accomplishments mean that my life is so full or rich? While in prison, Kelly made and maintained deep friendships, did important and meaningful work, and grew spiritually and emotionally. She had a true sense of purpose. Probably, in some ways, Kelly was freer than many of us. Still, because she had *stayed put* while I had lived a life of, at the very least, *motion,* I couldn't help but lament that her confinement had frozen her in time and deprived her of the life moments, stages, and choices that most of us take for granted.

Despite the life she made for herself in prison, Kelly had a harsh view of her years behind bars. As she wrote in 1999, "I thank God I was not given the death penalty or I could have been put to death by now. However, when a person is serving life, it is a *slow* death. The emotions slowly begin to die along with the physical body as it ages." Kelly felt forgotten by the world, as if she had simply disappeared.

There was a lot to talk about that first meeting. We talked and reminisced and planned strategy. The students were delighted with Kelly, and she with them. Kelly was remarkably open and warm. She didn't seem to mind that so many students had wandered in and out of her life over the years. She was glad to make new friends, and kept blessing us for coming.

Together we created a list of tasks—some having to do with prison life and some having to do with her case. We set a timetable for ourselves, so Kelly would know that there was an end to what we were doing and could feel a degree of control.

Over the next several months, we carried out these tasks. We contacted eyewitness Robert Hyland and the judge who had presided over the case and arranged to meet with them. We attempted to contact others: John Scholl; Scholl's former partner, who was now a judge; the defense investigator who worked on Kelly's case; Billy Ronald's lawyer; the police and prosecutor involved in the prosecution; and people who knew Kelly while she was in Utica. We tried to find William Sullivan, the man we believed was with Billy Ronald Kelly when he committed the crime. We drafted a careful letter to the parents of the young man who had been killed.

Scholl had been helpful during the federal appeals process and was glad to hear someone was working on Kelly's case. He had already sent Claudia his files but said he'd be happy to do whatever else he could. The case still plagued him. (Scholl died of a heart attack a few years after I resumed work on Kelly's case. He was 68. He never saw her free.)

Finding many of the others was difficult. The events of the case and the trial had occurred more than 20 years before. Memories had faded. Many people had retired and moved, and we couldn't find them. The defense investigator was semi-retired and was happy to talk to us, but couldn't remember much. Billy Ronald's lawyer was living on a boat somewhere in the Caribbean. Every single one of the police officers who had worked on the case was retired or dead. Although Kelly's judge, now elderly, was happy to meet with us, he kept asking what the name of the case was. The prosecutor who had tried Kelly's case had left the district attorney's office years before and had been disbarred for an ethical breach while in private practice. No one knew where he was.

Eyewitness Robert Hyland had become old and feeble since the trial. He was in his early 80s, but looked ancient. He agreed to speak with us, but he wasn't sure he could be helpful. He said his memory wasn't much good anymore, he had heart problems, and he had just gotten out of the hospital.

Most of our letters went unanswered.

The students and I took a two-day trip to upstate New York. The most important meeting was with Robert Hyland. We had high hopes, which we tried to curb. Still, over the course of the several-hour drive, we couldn't help but fantasize. A few years earlier, Sister Antonia, the Bedford Hills nun who had become Kelly's godmother, had visited Robert Hyland, and he had admitted feeling pressured to identify Kelly at trial. Sister Antonia had drafted an affidavit based on her visit. What would happen if Hyland went further and expressed misgivings about his identification? What if he admitted that he never had a good look at the person in the car at the Seaway station, that it could well have been a man, and he identified Kelly only because the police told him she was a prime suspect? Could we get a new trial on this basis? Could we get the police to reopen the case? Might this at least help in a clemency petition?

We were wise to keep our hopes in check, because Robert Hyland gave us nothing. It was difficult to get him to focus enough to answer the questions we put to him and difficult to understand his answers. He was on oxygen and apparently had had a stroke in addition to heart problems. He was happy for the attention and company but confused about his own role in the case. He stuck to the story he'd told at trial and denied having any second thoughts about it. He admitted something new—that he had attended the dead boy's wake—but denied that this had any impact on him as a witness. He spent most of his time talking about how sure he was of his identification of Billy Ronald. He said he felt sorry for Kelly, for how long she'd been locked up.

Hyland's daughter was not happy about our visit. When she phoned the nurse who was caring for her father and learned that we were there, she demanded to speak to the person in charge. After I got on the phone, she immediately threatened to call the police. She said her father was ill and frail and if he died, I would be responsible. I wasn't happy about this—I looked over at Hyland and quickly calculated the chances of his dying right then and there, which I supposed was *possible*—but I stood my ground. I said her father knew who we were and why we were there, had agreed to talk to us, and she could call the police if she wished.

The students were impressed with the way I handled the daughter. I told them I was more nervous than I sounded, but the more self-righteous and shrill the daughter had been, the bolder I became. Nevertheless, I was glad that Hyland was still alive when we left.

We went to the crime scene and looked around. We then went to the courthouse and dug up all the old documents in the case, in-

cluding some things we had never seen before—crime-scene photographs, the autopsy report, police reports documenting the
months of investigation before suspicion focused on Billy Ronald
Kelly, mug shots of Billy Ronald Kelly and Patsy Kelly Jarrett, press
accounts of the crime and trial, and a jury list. We were especially
happy to come upon the list of names and addresses of prospective
jurors from which the jury was selected because such lists were no
longer public information in New York.

Unfortunately, the letters we sent to jurors yielded only two re-
sponses, neither of which was terribly useful.

Surprisingly, the most hopeful moment of that trip was a meeting with a sergeant in the state police force. Although at first he
seemed only mildly interested in our visit—he was more enter-
tained by the sudden appearance of a group from Harvard than
concerned about an alleged miscarriage of justice—by the end of
our time with him, he seemed genuinely willing to work with us.
Youthful and engaged, he considered himself part of the new breed
in policing. He agreed that one-witness identification cases were
troubling. He said there was no worse nightmare for a police officer than helping to convict the wrong person.

The sergeant knew the whereabouts of the officers who
worked on the case back in the early 1970s and said he'd be willing
to help track down William Sullivan. He also said he would be willing to reopen the case if Kelly took and passed a polygraph exam.
He suggested an experienced and well-known polygraph examiner,
Richard O. Arther, who had trained many New York State police
officers.

In other words, if he believed that Kelly was telling the truth
about her innocence, he would help us.

Kelly was a nervous wreck about taking a polygraph exam. I didn't blame her. After nearly 20 years of imprisonment—of struggling daily to make sense of what had happened to her—a *machine* was going to determine once and for all whether she had been telling the truth about her innocence. She wanted to know why she should trust a machine, especially one operated by someone recommended by the police. She pointed out that machines don't always work and she might be really anxious during the exam. Also, she now knew so much about the evidence in the case. Might this might have an effect on the outcome? Mostly, Kelly was concerned about what would happen if for some reason she didn't pass. How public would the results be if they were bad? But she was also worried about how I would feel about her and how she would feel about herself.

Kelly's first concern about disclosure of results was easy to address. From a strategic point of view, she had nothing to lose by taking a polygraph. If she didn't pass, no one would ever have to know because the results of a polygraph conducted in the course of defense investigation are protected by lawyer-client privilege. So, even if the results were not what we hoped they would be, she'd be no worse off than she already was. But her other concern was not so easy. From an emotional point of view, there was a lot to lose.

I told Kelly we needed to do it. The polygraph could be enormously helpful, and, whatever happened, she was not going to lose my support. Although I knew we couldn't count on the police to vindicate Kelly, we had to take the sergeant up on his offer. At the very least, we would get some help locating Billy Ronald's former lover. At best, we'd have a positive polygraph result and local law enforcement on our side.

With financial assistance from the clinic, we hired Richard Arther, the polygraph examiner the sergeant had suggested. Arther had conducted polygraph training for many state, county, and federal law enforcement agencies, including the United States Army, Coast Guard, Customs Service, and Marine Corps. He had been the Chief Polygraph Consultant to the United States House of Representatives Assassination Committee, which investigated the murders of both John F. Kennedy and Martin Luther King. Arther would be assisted by his daughter, Catherine Arther, who was an experienced examiner in her own right. Catherine was president of the New York State Polygraphists and secretary of the New Jersey Polygraphists.

With her heart pounding—and mine too—Kelly took the polygraph exam on November 22, 1996, in one of the lawyer interviewing rooms at the prison. The examination was thorough and professional. To Kelly's relief and joy, shortly after administering the exam, the Arthers concluded that she "was telling the truth when she denies any involvement in the crime for which she was convicted." The Arthers detected no signs of deception whatsoever. Not only did Kelly pass the polygraph exam; her performance in it revealed the strongest indication of truth telling.

For Kelly, the polygraph results were a long-awaited vindication. Suddenly, after all those years, there was something to corroborate her claim of innocence. In the absence of a clear alibi, which had been impossible to establish because of the long delay between crime and arrest, she had never been able to prove that she was not at the Seaway station when the crime occurred. Now it wasn't just her word anymore. Now she could say to the world—to

the prison superintendent, the corrections staff, the other inmates, the governor of New York—I've been telling the truth, I
was wrongly identified, I've been locked up all these years for no
reason. Now she could say to her family and friends and lawyers:
"See, you were right to believe in me."

It must be said that the sergeant did keep his word: He took
another look at the case. But what he saw was the most complicated, least flattering truth.

He saw a couple who robbed and killed their way up and down
the East Coast.

He said, "Look, it would be one thing if it had just been the
Sherrill case. Maybe I could believe that your client was an unwitting accomplice if it were one time. But we're talking about
New York, Virginia, Pennsylvania, and Vermont." He said, "I
don't believe for one second that your client could be so naive
that she had no idea what was going on. No one could be that
naive."

After poring through the police files, the sergeant came away
horrified by the other similar offenses he found there. As bad as
the Hatch murder was, he now believed there were four such brutal crimes, with four victims—all the handiwork of the same perpetrators. (He did not mention the Edmonton, Canada, case that
we had come upon in the police reports. Probably he saw that Edmonton was nearly in British Columbia, more than 2,000 miles
away.) The sergeant believed that, during the summer of 1973, Billy
Ronald and Kelly went on a killing spree.

The sergeant recounted the facts of the Pennsylvania and Vermont crimes, which we knew about from the police investigation
running sheet. But while we had relied on the fact that neither the
fingerprints nor the description of the perpetrators in the Pennsyl-

vania and Vermont cases matched those in New York, the sergeant emphasized the similar details of the crimes.

The Phoenixville, Pennsylvania, case happened on July 25, a couple of weeks before the Sherrill case. Like the Sherrill case, it was a daytime robbery and murder in which the victims' body was found facedown in a back room, limbs bound with Johnson & Johnson brand adhesive tape. Like the Sherrill case, the victim was stabbed in the back as well as the throat. Again, a blue car was observed at the scene, and the perpetrator likely served customers during or after the crime.

Phoenixville is only a five-hour drive from Utica.

The White River Junction, Vermont, crime happened on July 31, a few days before Sherrill, and also involved a young victim—an 18-year-old college student working at his brother-in-law's Esso station. But unlike the New York, Virginia, and Pennsylvania cases, the young man survived and told a harrowing tale. A man with a southern accent and a sawed-off shotgun had forced him into a back room, bound his hands with adhesive tape, shot him in the back, and cut his throat. The young man managed to telephone for help before passing out.

White River Junction is only a four-hour drive from Utica, on the other side of the Adirondacks. The victim in that case said his assailant drove off in a blue car with North Carolina plates, accompanied by a woman.

The sergeant believed that Billy Ronald and Kelly had done the Pennsylvania crime on the way up to Utica, the Vermont crime while they were living in Utica, the New York crime as they were about to leave, and the Virginia crime on the way back down to High Point. He pointed out that both Phoenixville and White River Junction were easily accessible from major highways.

The sergeant was convinced that Kelly was with Billy Ronald for all of these crimes: It was her car, they were traveling companions, and she had admitted being with him during the Virginia murder. He dismissed the theory that Billy Ronald's companion had been an effeminate man. He thought Kelly was lucky to have received such generous treatment in Virginia, and lucky that Vermont and Pennsylvania lacked the evidence to make a case against her and Billy Ronald.

I tried to present a different slant. It wasn't simply that there was a lack of evidence connecting Billy Ronald and Kelly to Pennsylvania and Vermont; the forensic evidence and witness descriptions did not match Billy Ronald and Kelly. The Vermont victim described his assailant as a 24-year-old white man with short curly blond hair, nothing at all like Billy Ronald. The Vermont victim described his attacker's female companion as tall and dark, again not consistent with petite, light-complexioned Kelly. Although the victim said he saw North Carolina plates on a blue car, he could only describe the car in very general terms, was not sure about the make or model, and said the car was older than Kelly's 1970 Road Runner, which was in nearly mint condition. (Had I blocked out the part about North Carolina plates? My heart sank when he mentioned them.)

I said there were many unsolved crimes and, as the sergeant knew, single-attendant gas stations in remote areas were frequent crime targets. I also suggested that there was nothing terribly distinctive about the manner in which any of these crimes were carried out. Binding a victim in the course of a robbery was not unusual. The use of a knife or gun in the course of a homicide was not unusual.

I tried to reason with the sergeant, using geography. I said it seemed unlikely that Phoenixville, which is near Philadelphia, would have been on the route Billy Ronald and Kelly took from High Point to upstate New York. The much more direct route would have been through Harrisburg. There would have been no reason to go as far east as the Philadelphia metropolitan area. Moreover, by all accounts, Billy Ronald and Kelly left High Point in early- to mid-July, and the Pennsylvania crime happened in late July, after they had already spent a night or two in Herkimer. The prosecution's own witnesses provided those dates. The sergeant was unmoved. I pointed out that White River Junction, Vermont, is more than 200 miles from Utica, off the beaten path in general, and certainly off any route Billy Ronald and Kelly would have taken to or from Utica. The sergeant remained unmoved. He believed there was plenty of evidence to support his view that these crimes were the work of Billy Ronald, and it took no leap of faith to assume Kelly was with him.

When we asked Kelly about whether it was possible that she had been in the car when Billy Ronald robbed and killed in Pennsylvania and Vermont, she said no. She said they did travel through parts of Pennsylvania in early July—weeks before the Phoenixville crime—but nothing unusual happened on the ride up. She was emphatic that she had never been to Vermont. She and Billy Ronald did not drive through Vermont on the way up, they took the same basic route back down, and she went on no road trips with him during the time she was living in Utica.

The sergeant said he just could not believe Kelly, and that's what it came down to. He appreciated the fact that we had taken his advice about the polygraph examination. He had a lot of respect for Richard Arther. But there were just too many crimes. After confirming the rumors we had heard that Billy Ronald's erstwhile boyfriend William Sullivan had died of AIDS, he said he had no interest in helping Kelly.

Kelly was devastated. She had placed her hopes in the police. Then she got mad. "That sergeant lied to you," she said. "He never meant to look into my case." She said, "I don't care whether the sergeant believes it or not, I am sickened by Billy Ronald's vicious conduct and I had absolutely no idea at the time that he was doing anything like that. Maybe I was stupid. God knows I was naive. I admit I made a big mistake in associating with Billy Ronald. Maybe I deserve to be punished for that. But haven't I been punished enough?" When I suggested to Kelly that the sergeant was bound to see the facts of her case through his own lens—one skewed toward law enforcement—she was not moved. She wrote in December 1996, "I want you to understand how hurt, disappointed and disgusted I am over the state trooper's offer to reopen my case should I pass the Arthers' polygraph. The state trooper did not keep his word to you."

I told Kelly we had to forget about the sergeant and move forward. But during my dealings with the police sergeant, it became clear that he was privy to information I lacked. Using the Freedom of Information Act, I wrote to the Oneida County District Attorney's Office and the New York State Police and requested all police and related materials connected to the Hatch murder.

When I received the fresh batch of reports, I could see why the sergeant had been unsympathetic. There was new stuff in there, and none of it was good. It turned out that Billy Ronald had done some talking when he was locked up in Virginia: He had bragged about his murderous exploits in detail. Two jailhouse informants were able to provide chilling accounts of a multiple-state killing spree. The details matched the crimes in New York, Pennsylvania, and Vermont. Worse, according to the informants, Billy Ronald had claimed to have an accomplice, a North Carolina woman named Patsy Kelly Jarrett.

I felt like throwing up.

A former Virginia cellmate of Billy Ronald's said that Billy Ronald had talked about killing five gas station attendants during robberies. He claimed that Billy Ronald specifically mentioned cutting the throat of a young teenager near Utica, New York, after he taped up his hands and feet. He also told of cutting a gas station attendant's throat in Pennsylvania and shooting a gas station attendant with a shotgun and then cutting his throat somewhere in New England. This same inmate, who was serving a 45-year sentence for murder, offered to testify against Billy Ronald and Kelly in New York State in exchange for a shorter prison sentence. He said that Billy Ronald had told him that he was accompanied by Patsy Kelly Jarrett of High Point, North Carolina, when he killed the young gas station attendant during a robbery near Utica. He also said that the two used Kelly's blue Plymouth Road Runner to commit these crimes.

Billy Ronald's cellmate and codefendant in the prison murder case told authorities that Billy Ronald was upset when he learned that he had been indicted for the New York murder along with Patsy Kelly Jarrett. This inmate, who was serving time for robbery, said that Billy Ronald was afraid that Kelly might talk and implicate some other male.

In addition, there were a couple of old police reports from High Point, North Carolina. They revealed that Billy Ronald had been a suspect in a 1973 burglary of a truck leasing company and was being looked at for other crimes as well. The police believed that Billy Ronald left town in July to avoid the law, and Kelly knew about his problems.

I had a spasm of doubt. I felt shaken by what the informants said. It was painful to see Kelly's name mentioned in connection with other crimes, no matter the source. The details offered up by the first informant were in sync with the Pennsylvania and Vermont crimes; it was easy to see why the sergeant might have credited his account despite the lack of a fingerprint match and other discrepancies. Both informants mentioned Kelly specifically.

But jailhouse informants, or snitches, are, above all, salesmen. Motivated by self-interest, the information they seek to sell is often unreliable. Indeed, false testimony by informants is a significant factor in wrongful convictions. One thing in the informant statements rang particularly false: Why would a jailhouse informant who had never met Kelly be able to relay her full name—Patsy Kelly Jarrett—to the police? Surely Billy Ronald wasn't using Kelly's full name with a random cellmate. This had to have come from the police, who had an interest in tying Kelly to Billy Ronald's crimes. Sadly, sometimes police officers who are determined to prove a crime resort to orchestrating witness statements.

I had to do what I had told Kelly to do: move forward. There was nothing to be gained from going over and over the police investigation or having further conversations with the sergeant. The Virginia case said it all for him: If Kelly was in the car in Virginia, she was in the car the other times too.

The bottom line was that we would get no further help from the police and there was nothing I could do about it.

I consulted a number of experienced appellate lawyers who confirmed that without newly discovered evidence (we had none) or clear incompetence by Kelly's trial lawyer (there was none), Kelly had no further legal avenues. Clemency was the only option. A strong clemency petition would require us to:

1. Contact people who might have helpful information about the case.

2. Contact people who might write letters of support.

3. Collect Kelly's prison records.

4. Have Kelly draft a personal statement.

5. Prepare a memorandum in support of clemency.

6. Obtain helpful publicity for Kelly in order to generate public support.

Letters that had been sent to the Hatch family and to several friends of Kelly's from her days in Utica went unanswered.

The students and I learned that Billy Ronald had contracted the HIV virus in prison. We wrote him a letter telling him that Kelly had been taking care of prisoners with AIDS. We said it wasn't too late to tell the truth about the Sherrill crime and asked to meet with him. He responded with one terse line: "I decline your invitation and wish you luck in your endeavors." I was disappointed. It wasn't that anything Billy Ronald said—even if he were to completely exonerate Kelly—would make a difference. But he had been helpful in the past. I told the students that prison seldom brings out the best in people, and at least we had the previous affidavit.

We were essentially back where we had started: Kelly was a convicted murderer with a strong claim of innocence seeking executive clemency from a governor—Republican George Pataki had since taken office—who would be loath to grant it. Although Pataki had proposed some criminal justice reforms, such as reducing the excessively long sentences that were part of the Rockefeller drug laws, he also wanted to abolish parole. He was strongly opposed to parole for anyone convicted of a violent crime.[23]

Although the process of preparing and filing a clemency petition was affirming in some ways for Kelly—the petition laid out a
convincing claim of innocence, and the accompanying letters of
support were a concrete reminder that many people believed in
her—she despaired that anything would ever come of it.

I despaired too.

~

And then there is the question of faith. Although Kelly struggled with hope, she had boundless faith. Faith—in God and in
Jesus—sustained and comforted her, and provided moments of
serenity. It helped her come to terms with her plight. It kept her
going.

The longer Kelly was incarcerated, the more faithful she became. She displayed her Catholic faith quietly through prayer,
Bible study, and private contemplation. She was devoted—she attended mass daily, observed Catholic ritual, and felt Jesus' presence
in her life—but in a soft-spoken way. She never proselytized or
preached. Although Kelly sometimes decried the injustice and im-
perfection of the system, I never once heard her rail at God. I
never once heard her question Jesus or God's existence. I never
once heard her say her faith was being tested.

Indeed, she seemed to become increasingly beatific, saintly
even. She laughed at this observation when I shared it and then
dismissed it. She said she was far from saintly, that I was being
ridiculous. But she emanated goodness and humility. Where she
had once been playful and occasionally mischievous, she was now
solemn and introspective. Her voice had a gentler timbre, and the
cadence of her speech was slower.

Though I respected it, I couldn't understand this faith of hers. It's not that I am completely without what might be called faith: I have my own peculiar way of grappling with the great unanswerable questions and an inchoate but deep desire for connectedness and meaning. Mostly I'm terrified of death and would prefer to think there was something out there. I suppose this is why many people turn to faith. But Kelly's faith was so strong and enduring, and so unquestioning. She just *believed.*

The unquestioning part doesn't work for me.

Sometimes I was exasperated by Kelly's faith. Yes, it sustained her all those years, but it also led her to rely on "God's will" on a number of inconvenient occasions. The worst was when she put her faith in God and went forward with the federal appellate process rather than taking the plea for time served. Could there be a more disastrous example of misguided faith? What made Kelly think that God had anything to do with the Court of Appeals for the Second Circuit? Since that court's decision, she had come to believe that God had a purpose for her in prison, to tend to the sick and needy. Well, maybe so, but would God have any objection to her tending to the sick and needy *outside* prison?

Kelly would not have liked to know that her faith annoyed me. I can understand why. Her belief had provided comfort and kept her company over the years in a way that nothing else could have. It got her through those first nights and the many that followed. When I first contacted polygraph examiner Arther about Kelly's case, he wondered how an innocent person could still be in her right mind—sane enough to take a polygraph exam—after 20 years of wrongful incarceration. He was immediately reassured when he learned that Kelly had become religious.

Thankfully, Kelly's faith did not stop her from being human, and occasionally she got frustrated and even angry. Sometimes she was angry at me—for raising her hopes and wasting her time and, though she would never say it, for *failing her*. Sometimes her faith and her hope were at odds, the one sustaining and the other threatening to unravel her. At different points, Kelly expressed her anger and frustration by telling me to withdraw the clemency petition. This was her way of managing expectations and protecting herself from disappointment. She wrote in July 1996: "Clemency is a waste of your time. Pataki does not give clemency to anyone convicted of felony murder." In June 1998 she wrote: "When my father died last year, I asked Father O'Shea the priest here to call you and stop the clemency because I only did that to be able to see my father before he died."

But sometimes Kelly would let her faith ignite her hope. In October 1997 she wrote: "Sister Antonia said that she did not think I would be granted clemency and that they probably won't even bother to read the petition. Where is her faith? I will keep my faith anyway."

At such times I would get hopeful too. The clemency petition was seven inches thick and filled with important information. Kelly called it a masterpiece. It was a thorough and persuasive plea for her release. I couldn't help but feel hopeful: How could anyone read the petition and fail to be moved? I figured someone in the Pataki administration would read it and be won over. Someone would agree that Kelly had served enough time.

It felt silly being hopeful—and dangerous, especially for Kelly—but familiar. Hope had always been a good motivator for me. How could I not believe in my own efforts when believing in them had often worked in the past? I might not have labored so hard on the petition if I believed there was absolutely no hope. I began to think that maybe I could work a miracle. So long as the "jury" was still out (it took the clemency bureau almost two years before ruling on that first petition), there was still hope.

But I knew deep down that, no matter how much I wanted to, I wasn't going to rescue Kelly. It would take a whole lot more than me. The reality was that Kelly was probably going to be locked up for many more years and there was nothing, *nothing* I could do about it. I hated this reality. I hated whatever divine force caused this horrible chain of events to happen to Kelly and rendered me powerless to do anything about it.

~

That first lawyer-drafted clemency petition was denied on July 21, 1998. The letter to Kelly from James Murray, director of the New York State Executive Clemency Bureau, consisted of three short sentences:

> I regret to inform you that, after a careful review of your case, it has been determined that there is insufficient basis to warrant the exercise of the Governor's clemency powers. A grant of executive clemency involves intervention in the normal course of the criminal justice process. Such action constitutes extraordinary relief and is taken in only the most compelling of circumstances.

Under New York clemency procedures, we had to wait a year after the denial of clemency before filing another petition.

Chapter 4

Freedom

More time passed. Kelly got older. I got older too.

Every couple of years after that first denial I filed a new clemency petition, updating and adding letters of support, inserting new prison records, adding new research on eyewitness identification, revising and polishing my legal memorandum, and reworking Kelly's statement. Every couple of years the petition would be denied. I created a file for the one-page form letters, which I optimistically labeled "Correspondence with the Clemency Board." I hoped that one day there might be some actual correspondence.

Over the years Kelly's supporters changed jobs, retired, or moved, but I managed to track them down. I was like a ruthless reunion organizer without any cheerful gossip about who had recently divorced or had "work done." Kelly's supporters were always eager to hear whether there had been any progress in her case. I hated having to report that there was little.

I was tempted to resubmit the original petition with a new cover sheet and a couple of new letters of support. Nobody seemed to be reading it so what difference did it make? But I couldn't do it. At the very least, I wanted Kelly to know that I continued to work on her case and would put together the best possible argument for her release.

Some of Kelly's supporters died. Because they would have wanted me to do so, I kept their original letters in the petition. There was the especially poignant letter from Kelly's father, written in a shaky hand shortly before he died. When new policies prohibited prison staff from writing letters of support for prisoners seeking parole or clemency, I kept their letters in the petition as originally dated.

It seemed the clemency petitions would be denied no matter how carefully put together, no matter how thick. What I needed was *access*. I needed to make contact with someone in the governor's office who either made the clemency decisions or had that person's ear: I needed an audience with someone in power.

After the first clemency petition was rejected in 1998, I called the head of the New York State Clemency Bureau. I wasn't sure I'd be allowed to talk to him, because a student had managed only a brief conversation with a subordinate a couple of years before. But I gave it a try. Suddenly there he was, live, on the phone. I instantly regretted that I hadn't tried calling before submitting that petition. I introduced myself as Patsy Kelly Jarrett's lawyer. He said, "Oh yes, I've read your petition." He was friendly. We chatted. It turned out that he, too, had attended NYU Law School. We both spoke fondly of our alma mater. I thought, *Wow, this is great. He'll remember me. All politics is local.* I asked whether he had any advice, whether there was something else I should be doing on Kelly's behalf. He said some nice things about the petition, that it was thorough and well put together. But he also said it was a serious crime, and Kelly's escapes didn't help. He wasn't willing to say more. He encouraged me to keep submitting.

After George Pataki became governor, I tried to contact his wife, Libby. I heard that she had an interest in women in prison and had been instrumental in the release of a battered woman who had killed an abusive husband. I talked to a couple of her assistants and, on their advice, wrote a letter to New York's first lady, but got no reply. Follow-up efforts were equally unsuccessful.

I contacted a high-ranking lawyer in the criminal division of the New York State Attorney General's Office, the wife of a college classmate. The Attorney General's Office had represented the State of New York at the federal habeas proceedings. I felt a little uneasy exploiting that connection, but my classmate was now a law professor and friend whose scholarship focused on social justice. How could I not ask?

The wife took my call, listened to what I had to say, and agreed to pull the case file to see whether she might be helpful. She made no promises—even liberal-leaning prosecutors married to liberal-leaning law professors are noncommittal—but said she'd call me back. She did, with a depressing response: She said there was nothing helpful in the file and her office had no doubt about Kelly's guilt.

No doubt? Oh, for God's sake. It must be nice to have no doubt, *none whatsoever.* Meanwhile, I'm in doubt reading a menu. I end up regretting whatever I order. I'm drenched in doubt buying a pair of shoes. Something is always not quite right. A friend once dubbed me the Princess and the Pea. But this prosecutor had no doubt about a one-witness identification case.

I found out that Sister Antonia had been a parochial school teacher before going into prison ministry and had taught Governor Pataki's chief counsel. She was thinking about contacting him about Kelly, and I urged her to do so. Unfortunately, he wasn't helpful either.

We took a different tack. Claudia Angelos had gone to college and law school with Senator Charles Schumer of New York. I was friendly with Schumer's chief counsel, a former Washington, D.C., public defender. Between the two of us, I figured we might get Schumer to put in a word for Kelly with the Pataki administration. My friend was happy to help but wasn't sure what influence the Democratic senator had with the Republican governor. I don't think Claudia ever contacted Schumer though I'm sure she meant to do it. It was hard for her to think about Kelly.

I contacted Colorado congresswoman Diana DeGette, a law school classmate who had also been in the clinic. In fact, DeGette was with me when I met with Billy Ronald back in law school. Since she had no question about Kelly's innocence back then, I figured she'd be happy to write a letter for the clemency petition.

I couldn't get her to talk to me. She sent a message through an aide that she was sorry but couldn't get involved. How could writing a letter of support for a woman who had served more than 20 years based on dubious eyewitness testimony pose a threat to DeGette's political career? It wasn't even a Colorado case. I tried a few other times over the years—usually after receiving a campaign fundraising letter—with no luck.

I talked with another former clinic student, someone who had worked on Kelly's case after I did and was now an accomplished lawyer and lobbyist. She remembered Kelly well and was happy to hear of my efforts. She wanted to help and suggested that her husband, the head of an influential public interest organization, might also be helpful. I invited them both to brunch. The husband had some good ideas about media attention, but nothing came of it. Together with my partner Sally, the former student arranged to meet with staff members from the offices of both New York senators. Unfortunately, nothing came of that either.

There was the occasional breakthrough. United States Magistrate Judge Michael H. Dolinger, the author of the 1986 decision overturning Kelly's conviction, agreed to write in support of clemency, an extraordinary thing for a sitting judge to do. His letter stated that he stood by his decision: The witness's in-court identification was unreliable as a matter of law.

Over the years I tried hard to get Kelly's story told. No one had heard of her; no one knew of her plight. I felt certain that if people knew the facts of her case, they would feel as I did. If we reached enough people, we could make something happen.

I wanted a good print story more than anything else. A convincing newspaper or magazine article would be a useful organizing tool. If we got a good story in a reputable magazine with a high New York circulation—an accurate account of the case that also managed to capture Kelly as a person—we also might be able to attract other coverage. Although television had had the potential to draw the largest audience, it felt risky. Most television newsmagazines tended to be sensational, especially segments on crime. I didn't want a sensational account of Kelly's case, or worse, one that focused on the victim.

National Public Radio was also a consideration. I love NPR; I couldn't survive my rush-hour commute without it. I figured a good feature story—by Susan Stamberg, Lianne Hansen, Scott Simon—might be just the thing.

My first choice was a piece in *The New Yorker,* with the *New York Times Magazine* a close second. This was the best venue for a comprehensive story. Over the years I contacted countless writers. Several expressed interest. But they wanted a firm commitment from the magazine in order to say yes. I had an encouraging exchange with the editor of *The New Yorker.* We had a friend in common and I shamelessly used the connection. The editor was interested in "these kinds of stories" but wouldn't commit to anything without a proposal by a particular writer.

I wrote to writers whose work I admired. I contacted college classmates, law school classmates, the spouses of classmates, friends of friends of friends. I lost count of the people I contacted.

One of the problems was that Kelly's story had no ending. Without an ending, there was no clear narrative structure. There was only a beginning and endless middle.

Another problem was that Kelly's story wasn't easy to tell. It was too complicated to fit into a standard 15- to 20-minute television slot. The TV show *20/20* was attracted to the project but couldn't figure out how to do it. Neither could *Dateline NBC,* where I had a contact.

One journalist came through, a smart young *Boston Globe* reporter named Karen Avenoso. One of my Harvard students had told her about Kelly's case, and she was intrigued. Although the *Globe* wasn't exactly what we were looking for, it was in the Northeast and had a substantial readership. It was also the only real bite we'd had. After talking it over with Kelly, we signed on with Karen.

Karen spent lots of time with Kelly and me, separately and together. She read the trial transcript, court decisions, clemency petition, and police records. In 1997, only months after we had met, her story about my efforts to free Kelly was published as the cover story in the *Boston Globe Magazine*. It captured Kelly's earnestness and innocence and made a strong case for her release.

The *Globe* piece generated several months of supportive mail for Kelly and the usual pile of prisoner mail for me. It also lent credibility to our efforts—I included it in the clemency petition and in the collection of materials I sent around to potential supporters and media people—but it wasn't the breakthrough I had been hoping for.

Tragically, Karen died a year later of Ewing's sarcoma, a rare and virulent form of cancer usually found in children. She was diagnosed soon after the article came out. She was only 31 years old.

Some time after the *Globe* story, with the help of a friend who lived in Albany, I managed to interest an NPR reporter in upstate New York in Kelly's story. The reporter thought it would make a good radio piece. I was delighted. This would be the perfect target audience. I spent hours with this reporter, drove to the prison with her, arranged for a private interview with Kelly, and got permission for her to bring a tape recorder. She and Kelly hit it off. It turned out they were both devout Catholics. The reporter was moved by Kelly's enduring faith.

After reviewing all of the documents in the case and taking hours of interviews, however, the reporter called one day to say she was leaving NPR, quitting journalism, and moving to the Midwest. She was sorry she had never managed to pull the story together. She wished me and Kelly well and said that God would one day answer Kelly's prayers.

What is it with these religious people? I fumed. *God.*

More years passed with only the *Globe* story on record. It wasn't for lack of trying. Anytime I came across a sensitive criminal justice story, I contacted the writer. I became less discriminating. Anytime I came across a sensitive story about *anything*, I contacted the writer: writers of fiction and nonfiction, political writers and social commentators, even a couple of poets. I admit that I sometimes engaged in fantasy, like the time I wrote a letter to Dorothy Allison, the author of *Bastard Out of Carolina.*[1] In addition to being a National Book Award finalist, Allison was a southern, working-class lesbian. I thought she would do a great job with it, and it would then be made into a movie starring Amy Madigan as Kelly and Debra Winger as me. (Every Jewish woman I know wants Debra Winger to play her in a movie. I am realistic enough to know that Julie Kavner—Rhoda's sister, Woody Allen's business partner in *Hannah and Her Sisters,* and the voice of Marge Simpson in *The Simpsons*— was more likely to play me.) The resulting groundswell of support would ultimately lead to Kelly's release. I never heard back.

I sought out public relations firms. Some PR people expressed interest, but nobody was willing to actually do it.

Finally, I decided to write about Kelly myself, which I did in a short article in the *National Law Journal* in 1997. I wrote a longer article in the *Connecticut Law Review* in 2000 and another article in the *Notre Dame Journal of Legal Ethics* in 2004.

These were not mainstream publications, but I didn't have many options and this is where law professors publish. At least I was putting Kelly's story out there. Maybe someone would read about Kelly and offer help.

Amazingly, this happened. Pace University law professor Ben Gershman read the law review article and was stirred by it. A former New York prosecutor, he was aware of the dangers of eyewitness identification. He believed that, as a matter of ethics, prosecutors should not bring a case that is based on the uncorroborated testimony of a single eyewitness. Gershman wondered whether it might be helpful for Kelly to have a former prosecutor in her camp. He offered to meet her.

Ben spent several hours with Kelly and came away convinced of her innocence. He called and said, "She just has this innocence about her." "I know," I said. He said, "We have to get her out of there." "I know, I know," I said.

Ben's reaction reminded me of a letter I received from Jean Harris in the mid-1990s. She wrote: "You're absolutely right about Kelly's innocence. You have only to meet her to know she is incapable of even hurting anyone or committing any kind of crime." (Harris tried to get investigative journalist Dominic Dunne, whom she knew slightly, to write about Kelly. Nothing came of it.)

Ben wrote a strong letter of support for the clemency petition, expressing concern about Kelly's conviction from a prosecutorial perspective. Over time, he became an important consultant and confidant, and the link to the big break we so desperately needed. In the spring of 2003, he described Kelly's case to documentary filmmaker Ofra Bikel, who was just beginning work on a film on guilty pleas for the PBS television show *Frontline*. Ben also gave Ofra my name and suggested that I might want to call her. Ofra and I began to explore the possibility of including Kelly in her film.

༄

It is hard to say what exactly Kelly was feeling during those years. She seemed the same: alternately hopeful and discouraged. Remarkably, she was seldom despondent. Every once in a while she would throw up her hands and say it wasn't worth it—the effort, the emotion, the constant waiting—she should just do the time. I ignored her and carried on.

I had my own struggles with despondency. I had little to show for my ten years of work on Kelly's case. Yes, we had done some additional investigating, Kelly had taken and passed a polygraph exam, we had a lengthy and impressive-looking clemency petition, there were now a handful of published accounts of her case, she had a growing list of supporters, and she had a lawyer who was committed to her cause. But what good had it done? Not only was Kelly still in prison, I hadn't even been able to get her moved to the section of the prison reserved for well-behaved inmates. No matter how much time passed, no matter how many pleas I made or letters I wrote, it always came down to Kelly's escape attempts. It didn't matter that these were more than 20 years old and that she had been a model prisoner ever since.

I began to think of myself as the most devoted but least effectual lawyer on earth. If there was a category in the *Guinness Book of World Records* for "ineffectual lawyering," I could be a contender.

I began to think that I was the wrong person for this case. I was a trial lawyer, not an appellate lawyer. Trial work suits me: I have the attention span and stamina of a trial lawyer, and occasionally I win cases. The urgency of a trial—of preparing for it, being immersed in it, and, when all the evidence is in and closing arguments are over, awaiting the verdict—gets my juices flowing. A case usually goes to trial within a year of the arrest. It's over before you know it. Whatever the result, when one case is finished, you move on to the next. It's freeing. It's an exercise in letting go.

But Kelly's case threatened to go on *forever.* I would be her lawyer forever. I would be saddled with this case forever.

There was no letting go.

Over the years Kelly wrote me hundreds of letters. No matter what was going on in her case, no matter what disappointment or setback had just occurred, she was extravagant in her gratitude and praise. Nearly every letter began with her thanks to me for standing by her. Nearly every letter said how grateful she was to not be forgotten.

In 1993 she wrote: "I'm so happy to have you back in my life, Abbe. I will never forget you for not forgetting me."

In 1994 she wrote: "I don't know what I would do without your help, Abbe. I kept praying for help. Maybe that's why God sent you back to me. Maybe with your help I will make it out of this place."

In a 1995 letter she wrote: "I thank you from my heart for everything you do for me."

In a 1996 birthday card she wrote: "I want to tell you how much your friendship means to me. I thank God for your life each and everyday. I thank Him for your birthday. You are my strength and hope in a place of endless suffering. There are no words to express how much you mean to me as a person and as a friend. . . . Knowing that you care keeps me alive and able to say I love you on your birthday and always."

A few months later that same year, after having persuaded Kelly to take the polygraph exam and meet with journalist Karen Avenoso (something she resisted, partly because Karen had to reschedule her first visit at the last minute and word never reached Kelly, who waited all day in a borrowed silk blouse), things were somewhat tense, and she was not that happy with me. Still, she wrote: "I want to tell you that I'm very, very grateful for your concern about my life. I hope you don't think I resent anything you do for me. I've been living in hell for almost 20 years and there is nothing I cannot handle or deal with."

For my birthday in 1997 she wrote: "Wish I had a really nice card. You deserve the best, but being in here it's hard to get the kind of card I want for you. All I know is that because of your life, mine has become worth living even in a place like this."

In December 1997 she wrote, "My father died on December 10th at 4:00 A.M. I have waited 20 years to see my father. I haven't written to anyone until now. . . . I will miss my father's love . . . however, God will fill in the emptiness through you and other people who care."

In 1998, just after the denial of the first post-polygraph clemency petition, Kelly wrote: "There are no words to express how very grateful I am to you for your care and concern about my life. Please know in my heart there will always be a very special place for you."

There were also letters expressing frustration, indignation, and sadness. Sometimes she did so sardonically, like the words she scrawled at the top of a letter to me on April 24, 1997: "20 years in prison. Wish me a happy anniversary!" and sometimes more fiercely, like a letter she wrote in late 1998: "Abbe, I don't want to file another clemency. Sister Antonia says it is a waste of time. I want to bring this case to the media. I want my name cleared. I only did the clemency to be with my father, who has died like my mother, waiting for me to get out. I do not want the Governor's *mercy*. I want my name cleared."

There were periods when she told me to just be her friend and not her lawyer, because it wasn't worth my effort. In early 2002 she wrote:

I want you to just be my friend and forget the attorney stuff. It's all just too hard. Clemency is for a guilty person that the state decides to have "mercy" on. I do not want you to waste your valuable time on all the work because no one is reading it but us. By the way, congratulations on your win with the drug case. Abbe, you should spend your time on helping defend people that have a chance to *win*.

Kelly struggled with feelings of anger. She didn't want to be angry, but she couldn't help it sometimes. In early 1999 she wrote: "Abbe, every time I read this clemency petition you worked so hard on, and know in my heart it was *never even read,* I get very angry. I don't want their damn mercy. I want my mistaken conviction to be overturned. I pray a lot and, with God's help, it will be done." A few months later she wrote: "Abbe, your friendship means a lot to me and when I'm angry I feel comfortable to express it to you."

She struggled with feelings of sorrow, too. On March 24, 2001, she wrote: "Today is the anniversary of my mother's death and even though it was in 1990, the deep hurt and memory of not being able to be there with her and for her is always with me. It is like that for my father, too, gone since 1997."

But mostly Kelly was grateful. In 2000 she wrote: "I want to thank you for your concern about my life and your friendship throughout the years. Please also thank Sally for all she has done to help you help me." In 2001 she wrote, "I want to thank you from the bottom of my heart for caring about my life. Please know that I thank God for you everyday." In 2002 she wrote: "I love you very much and I'm grateful for all that you do for me throughout the years, and continue to do."

Every year I received a card from Kelly on the Jewish New Year, my birthday, Thanksgiving, Hanukah, Valentine's Day, Passover, and Mother's Day.

I pictured her going to the prison shop with the little money she squirreled away—from her three-dollar-a-week prison job and the generosity of friends and family—and picking out just the right card. She had to send away for those harder-to-find Jewish holiday cards. By and large, her taste was sentimental. But occasionally she sent something funny and contemporary—the kind of cards my friends and I might send each other.

Once she sent a *New Yorker* cartoon in which one snail says to another about a strangely similar-looking tape dispenser, "I don't care if she is a tape dispenser. I love her." Would everyone find this charming, or did Kelly and I share a peculiar sensibility? At the very least, she knew me well enough to know I'd appreciate it.

She put a lot of herself into those cards and letters, often covering every inch with her careful print. She was a good writer. I felt her in those letters: her trust, her need, her life ticking away.

How could I not continue to fight for Kelly's release? Who else did she have? Why practice law if not to represent someone like Kelly? The letters go on and on, a lifetime in letters.

Of course, we also had many phone conversations, made difficult by my court and class schedule, not to mention her lack of privacy, others clamoring for the use of the phone, and the ever-present background prison noise. Kelly almost always declared it was a "miracle" whenever she reached me in fewer than three tries. The calls were sometimes urgent and purposeful (about problems at the prison, family troubles, concerns about her case) and sometimes just to touch base. No matter what, Kelly's voice was full of love.

The in-person visits were almost always to introduce someone to Kelly—someone from the media, a lawyer interested in her case, a writer interested in her case, or a new student working on her case. Sometimes, when I felt that it had been too long between visits, I would take a drive to Bedford Hills on my own. I didn't like to visit without being able to bring news of an encouraging development, but sometimes all I brought was me.

Doing time became harder and harder as Kelly aged. She found it difficult to put up with the noise, the fights, the constantly changing prison staff, the petty dramas of prison life. During Kelly's incarceration, the U.S. prison population boomed—between 1977 and 2004, the total number of state and federal prisoners increased by nearly 400 percent, and the number of women prisoners rose by more than 750 percent[2]—and the boom was felt at Bedford Hills too. The population at Bedford became younger and more troubled. It was a more dangerous place, especially for a middle-aged woman who wasn't from the streets.

Once Kelly was viciously attacked by a younger inmate who thought Kelly had "disrespected" her. Kelly had no idea what the inmate was talking about; she made it a practice to mind her own business. Suddenly the inmate struck her with a metal bucket, causing her to fall down a flight of stairs. Kelly's nose was broken in the attack, and she lost sight in both eyes for several days because of swelling. Fortunately, she regained her vision and otherwise recuperated. But the attack frightened and angered her. "This is where I live," she said to me. "This is what I have to put up with day to day." The woman was sent to SHU (the segregated housing unit), but Kelly wasn't comforted. "She'll get out and blame me," she said. Kelly wanted to file a lawsuit against the prison for failing to protect her, but she didn't want to cause trouble for any guards.

Kelly's friends did their time and got out while she remained imprisoned. Nearly everyone she knew was on the Honors Floor, where they had greater freedom and privileges, while she remained in general population because of her escapes. Eventually she stopped making new friends. What was the point if she was just going to lose them? Kelly did make a few close friends over the years, and some kept in touch. But when people leave prison, they often want to get as far away as they possibly can.

As the years went on, Kelly became increasingly withdrawn. She turned inward. She refused to play on the prison baseball team, saying she had gotten too old. She refused to sign up for a writing class run by Eve Ensler, author of *The Vagina Monologues,* which was later the subject of a documentary film called *What I Want My Words to Say to You,* in which Marisa Tomei, Glenn Close, and Rosie Perez read the prisoners' work. Kelly said she didn't want to join the class because she didn't want to share her feelings. I tried to persuade her but she wouldn't budge.

In those last years in prison, Kelly had only one close friend in the prison: a woman convicted of killing several of her own babies. The friend was a nurse with no prior record who maintained that her babies had died of SIDS (sudden infant death syndrome). But the police, prosecution, and jury thought otherwise. All Kelly knew was she was a good person and a good friend.

Whenever I asked Kelly how she tolerated all those years of incarceration, how she slept at night, how she managed to find any kind of solace, she would answer, "God." I would persist. "But didn't you feel terribly lonely and frightened, especially at first?" "No," she would say, "because God was with me." I would say, "You must have had a place in your head where you lived to block out the prison—some childhood memory, a story, a fantasy." "No," she would say. "When I couldn't sleep I would read the Bible." "But," I asked, "how did you not lose all hope?" "I knew that Jesus would not forsake me," she said.

I realize it was impolite to press Kelly on this. I should have been glad that she found comfort in faith. But I had a hard time understanding it.

The spring of 2003 turned into summer. This was the summer I would come to regard as "the summer of the beginning."

Aside from making contact with filmmaker Ofra Bikel, the most significant event was meeting a writer and activist named Scott Christianson. I first came upon Scott in 2002. A friend who lives in Albany had gone to a reading of his book on the history of imprisonment in America, *With Liberty for Some,*[3] and bought it for me. The book jacket said the writer had been a high-ranking criminal justice official in the Cuomo administration. My eyes lit up.

It turned out that Scott was working on a book about wrongly convicted prisoners in New York and was interested in Kelly's story. The more I shared, the more concerned he was. But he wasn't just interested because of his own research. Scott understood the danger of a one-witness identification case. He understood the randomness of mistaken identification and the fact that what happened to Kelly could have happened to anyone. She was one more innocent person who got caught up in the criminal system and couldn't get out.

Like Ben Gershman, Scott did more than express concern. He wanted to meet Kelly. Not only was he interested in including her in his book, he wanted to help. We picked a day and arranged to meet at the prison. He would be driving from Albany, a two-hour drive at least.

I made the arrangements for Scott's visit, including having Kelly's prison social worker put him on the list as an approved visitor. I went a step beyond this to ensure that there were no glitches by getting the superintendent's permission. (It turned out Scott and prison superintendent Elaine Lord had known each other for years. In addition to traveling in similar criminal justice circles, they'd gone to college together.) I called the prison the day before the visit to make sure all the paperwork was in order.

So much for the best-laid plans. I was with Kelly for nearly an hour before I realized that something must have gone wrong. When I reached Scott on his cell phone he was killing time at a nearby coffee shop, hoping I would call. He had been turned away from the prison because his name was not on the list. He was good-humored about the runaround: "It's par for the course," he said. "They keep people like me out and people like Kelly in."

I managed to persuade a deputy superintendent that the visit was fully authorized and the superintendent would not be happy to learn that her old friend had been turned away. Soon Scott was inside meeting. Kelly was so pleased; you'd think I had brought the governor himself. Maybe she saw that occasionally I could accomplish something. Scott was worth the effort. He was perfect with Kelly. He listened respectfully as she told her story. When she was finished, he told her how sorry he was that this had happened to her. He offered to write about her in his newest book so more people would know of her struggle, and to work with me in the clemency effort. He told Kelly to list his home telephone number as an approved call so that she could call him collect whenever she wanted.

Scott agreed that we had to get Kelly's story out. He said he'd do his part in the new book and the speaking tour that would accompany its publication. As part of his work on wrongful convictions, he had helped bring about the release of a handful of prisoners and had learned some things in the process. He was happy to talk strategy. He was candid about not having the contacts in high places he used to have, but he knew people. He said I might want to get in touch with a legal aid lawyer named Sara Bennett, who had recently obtained clemency for another Bedford Hills prisoner.

I was open to this suggestion but wary. I had already reached out to a number of New York lawyers in my efforts on Kelly's behalf without success. Lawyers doing postconviction work seemed to have their own favorite clemency candidates and, because so few prisoners are ever granted clemency, it felt competitive.

Around the same time, my friend Danny Greenberg—then the director of the New York Legal Aid Society, and Sara Bennett's boss—also mentioned her. Danny knew about Kelly. He suggested that I join forces with the Legal Aid Society's fledgling Wrongful Convictions Unit, which Sara headed. In addition to wanting to help, he was looking for a case that might involve and rouse the legal aid board of directors. He wanted a project the board could feel good about and thought Kelly's case was a good fit. Several board members were well connected, he told me, and one had run the Criminal Justice Office in the Pataki administration. Though he encouraged me to go through Sara first, he was eager to sign on and would be happy to throw some resources my way.

This was irresistible. There were many impressive people on the legal aid board: I might finally have access to people with power. Moreover, two people I respected were telling me to contact Sara. The plan was that Danny would express interest in

Kelly's case to Sara and I would follow up by sending a letter and accompanying materials making the case for the Wrongful Convictions Unit's involvement.

I had my first real conversation with Sara that summer. She had read the materials I sent and was especially moved by the *Connecticut Law Review* essay. She said it captured her own experience like nothing she'd ever read. We talked and talked. It was like finding a long-lost friend. In fact, we did know lots of people in common, and, before going to law school, Sara had worked at the same progressive news service where I had once been a cartoonist.

I asked Sara if she was willing to help. She said she was. She agreed with Danny that Kelly's case might appeal to the legal aid board and was eager for the opportunity to work with board members.

Sara was a gifted organizer and wasted no time getting started. She began with that first phone call: She organized *me*. She said we needed to get going immediately: We needed a game plan and a schedule. We agreed to direct all our efforts for the end of December, only five months away. Christmas is clemency time, she said, and we have a lot to do between now and then. She began to divide tasks between us. She wanted a manageable packet of materials to send around, a press strategy, my available dates for a meeting with the legal aid board, dates for meetings with people from the Clemency Bureau and the governor's counsel, and a small, well-chosen group of Kelly's supporters to bring along to some of these meetings. She also wanted to meet Kelly as soon as she could.

Sara was excited about the prospect of Kelly being featured in Ofra Bikel's documentary. She knew and admired Ofra's work. As she was curious to see Ofra at work, to see how she managed to draw so much from the people she interviewed, I arranged to have both Sara and Ofra meet Kelly on the same day. I would go to New York, meet Sara in person over a cup of coffee, collect Ofra at her apartment, and drive them to Bedford Hills.

Ofra was not certain she would use Kelly; she needed to meet her and determine whether she would be compelling on screen. She thought Kelly's story was interesting and found her refusal to plead guilty even when offered her freedom especially intriguing.

The meeting went well, I thought. Kelly was Kelly: a little too grateful, a little too obedient, a little too pious, but everything about her shouted innocence and basic *goodness*. She and Sara seemed to hit it off. Kelly liked it that Sara had represented a friend of hers who had been released from Bedford a few months before. She liked it that Sara had been to the Greenwich Village club where Kelly had tended bar during the weeks she was a fugitive. I wanted Ofra to have more time with Kelly without anyone else present—to draw her out more, to get to know her better—but I thought Kelly had won her over too.

On the drive back to Manhattan, I asked Ofra what she thought of Kelly. She said, "Frankly, I couldn't find her." This wasn't what I was hoping for. I said, "I guess I know what you mean: All those years of incarceration have taken their toll, and Kelly is locked up emotionally as well as physically. But didn't you like her?" She said, "Of course I liked her. Who wouldn't like her? But she is all piety and submissiveness. I couldn't find Kelly; I couldn't find the person." I said, "Please don't make any decisions. Let me talk to Kelly. This is a really good story, too good to pass up, and it's perfect for your film. There's more to Kelly than what you saw. I've known her for years. There is still a person there, honestly. She just needs to show you."

Ofra said she'd think about it. Maybe she'd go back to the prison in a couple of weeks by herself. She would see.

I talked to Kelly the next day. She immediately asked what Ofra thought and whether she would be included in the film. I told her what Ofra had said. Kelly was aghast. "She couldn't find me? She couldn't *find* me?" Kelly repeated. "I've spent 25 years buried alive in that prison. Of course she couldn't find me. The person I once was died a long time ago, and no one can find her, not even me." I said, "But Kelly, what about who you are now?" She said, "I don't let just anyone know who I am now. I need to protect myself. There's been so much loss." I said, "I understand. But we need this film." Kelly said, "Ofra needs to be more patient and I need to be more trusting. Then she'll find me."

I thought this was astute, and wrenching. I shared it with Ofra. I explained that Kelly and I had also figured out why she had been reticent in response to some of Ofra's questions, especially questions about the future. Thinking about the future is the hardest thing for Kelly because she believes she may spend the rest of her life in prison. She can't afford to picture a future if it's not going to happen. I told Ofra that Kelly also understood that there is a certain rote quality to the way she talks about the facts of her case. But she has been living with these facts for a quarter century—the trial transcripts, the appeals, the court decisions, the endless going over the facts with lawyers and law students—she has been pummeled by the facts.

Ofra seemed to find this conversation helpful, but she wasn't entirely convinced. She'd let me know.

I kept calling her until she said yes.

Shortly after my conversations with Kelly and Ofra, I received a letter from Kelly. She wanted to make sure I understood how she felt about Ofra's comment. She wrote:

Abbe, I need you to understand that the young woman I used to be—that young woman named Patsy—died in 1977. Patsy died and was buried alive in the prison system. It takes a while to die inside, it is a slow process that occurs when you're locked in a cage like an animal and forced to be away from people you love and care about. You learn that, in order to survive, you had better be tough. . . . You get into fights that no one even knows about, but you get strong, you get hard, you learn how not to cry and how not to show any kind of emotion (that is, if you want to survive). You're locked up with people who really did kill and they brag about it. You watch them leave and come back and leave again and you wonder why. And you feel angry that these people who are really dangerous get to leave and you have to stay. Your parents die and you can't even attend their funerals. You watch inmates' children grow up and have children of their own. Then you watch the grandchildren grow up. You hold women and watch them die of AIDS, cancer, and lupus, and you hope with all your heart that you will not die here, too. And then you realize that you're already dead—that you, the real you, isn't here anymore.

So, Abbe—Ofra did not see me because I am buried deep, so deep that I hope, should I even get the chance to walk out of this living hell, I can *come back*. Maybe being "free" around people who love me will bring my spirit alive again. I don't know.

I told Kelly I understood. I said I hoped I would be there when her spirit came alive again.

Meanwhile, Sara and I worked to get Kelly's case before the governor's counsel, who is as close as you can get to the governor himself when it comes to clemency, with much more clout than the clemency chief. She and I made a presentation before the legal aid board in September and specifically enlisted the board member who used to head the Criminal Justice Office as well as several other board members. We assembled the ideal team for an October meeting in Albany with staff attorneys from the Office of the Governor's Counsel: former prosecutor Ben Gershman, former criminal justice official Scott Christianson, polygraph examiners Richard and Catherine Arther, Sara, and me. When severe thunderstorms delayed the Arthers we proceeded without them. It was a good meeting. The attorneys seemed receptive.

A couple of hours later the Arthers had their own meeting with the same government attorneys. Richard Arther had become elderly and frail. It was not easy for him to travel. But he was determined to tell people in Albany what he thought about Kelly no matter how bad the weather was. He had conducted hundreds of polygraph examinations in his life. He had worked extensively with law enforcement agencies. Over the years, he had found few accused or convicted people to be telling the truth. He told those assembled that he could not convey strongly enough his belief in Kelly's innocence. Catherine added her agreement.

With the legal aid board member's help, we were granted a meeting with the governor's counsel himself, a not-yet–40-year-old lawyer who had been appointed counsel only a few months before. Because the board member knew the counsel personally, we felt that he should take the lead in the meeting. He was magnificent. He laid out the weaknesses in the case against Kelly, the problem with single eyewitness identifications, Kelly's long-standing claim of innocence and refusal to take a plea, Kelly's favorable polygraph exam, and the many years Kelly had been in prison even if, as the prosecution had maintained, she was in a car at the scene of the crime.

The governor's counsel listened to the presentation without interrupting, but as soon as the legal aid board member was finished he had the same old questions: What about Kelly's escapes? What about the fact that her car was used in the crime? What about the fact that she traveled with Billy Ronald Kelly in that car? What about the Virginia robbery and murder? What about Vermont and Pennsylvania?

We did our best to answer these questions, pointing out that traveling with Billy Ronald and letting him use her car did not make her an accomplice to murder. We noted that the State of Virginia, not known for being soft on crime, had determined that Kelly had nothing to do with the Virginia killing, that she was instead an unwitting bystander. We said there had never been any evidence tying Kelly to what happened in Vermont or Pennsylvania, that Kelly denied ever stepping foot in Vermont, and that these places were not en route to or from North Carolina.

The counsel seemed unmoved. He wanted to know why clemency, an extraordinary remedy, was necessary when Kelly would be eligible for parole in a year and a half. "Because she has already served 27 years for a crime she did not commit," we said. Moreover, we argued, parole at the first date of eligibility for a convicted murderer was far from certain.

We were elated when we received word that Kelly would appear before the clemency board in November. This was big. Maybe the governor's counsel had not been dead set against us. The only prisoners who got a hearing before the board were serious candidates for clemency. Kelly and I had never gotten this far before.

Kelly was a nervous wreck. Lawyers aren't allowed at clemency hearings, so Kelly would be on her own. She would have to speak for herself. What if she couldn't find the words?

Sara and I went into high gear, preparing Kelly in person and by telephone. We covered all the obvious issues: the seriousness of the Sherrill crime, the other crimes, Kelly's friendship with Billy Ronald, her escapes, where she would live and work if she were granted clemency, and what sort of support system she had outside the prison. We conducted practice sessions where Sara and I shot hard questions at Kelly as if we were hostile board members. If Kelly did well with us, she would do well with the real board.

Kelly had a particularly good answer to the question about where she would live and work. She would reside at the Mount St. Francis convent in Peekskill, New York, where Sister Antonia lived, and she would work in the convent infirmary. The Franciscan sisters would be her family and support system. Moreover, Kelly's transition from the strictly controlled prison environment to life on the outside would be eased by her choice of residence. What could be better for a parole board—a prisoner who wants to live in a convent! Kelly would go from one highly structured, all-female environment to another.

Fretting over her ability to say the right thing to the board, Kelly prepared a written statement. Sara and I talked her out of it. Kelly needed to be herself, she needed to be fresh. She needed to talk to the members of the board, not make a speech.

Kathy Boudin, the former member of the Weather Underground who spent 20 years at Bedford Hills for participating in a Brinks truck robbery that left one man dead, was released on parole in 2003. A few days before her release, knowing that Kelly was about to face the clemency board, she wrote a letter to Kelly:

> Dear Kelly. It is 2:20 A.M.—I'm burning the midnight candle. I write to tell you how, as I watched you in the yard tonight, you looked so young—your face was so youthful. And all I wanted to do was to tell you—I hope with all my heart that you make your . . . board. Please know that my energy will go with you as you approach your time. You are a really truly good person and I wish you all the best. Much love, Kathy.

During this same time period, we managed to get the press interested in Kelly's case. We even had a choice. There was a *New York Times* writer who had covered one of Sara's cases and was interested in Kelly's clemency effort. We had mixed feelings. The *Times* is the gold standard—it has clout—but we didn't trust this reporter. The last thing we needed was a negative story, one that emphasized the facts of the crime, or mentioned the similar crimes in Virginia, Vermont, and Pennsylvania.

An Associated Press writer in upstate New York named Michael Hill was also interested. He had heard about Kelly's case from an old friend of mine who also worked for the AP. There was something about him I liked. I checked out some other stories he had written and his approach felt right for Kelly. I was especially taken with a story he had written about David Kaczynski, the brother of Unabomber Theodore Kaczynski. His stories brought out the humanity of the players; they were not typical crime stories. I decided to go with the AP. Kelly agreed. Eventually, so did Sara.

The AP story was fine. It emphasized Kelly's avowed innocence, her long struggle for freedom, and my efforts on her behalf. Plenty of people read it. (Kelly and I both got an influx of mail as a result.) But the best part of the story was investigative. Michael Hill managed to make contact with Paul Hatch's mother, something I had tried to do over the years but had never accomplished. Mrs. Hatch told the reporter that Kelly had served enough time and she forgave her.

This was a huge development. It could make all the difference. *The victim's mother was not opposed to Kelly's release!* Surely this would help push the clemency board and the governor.

Meanwhile, Kelly appeared before the clemency board and called me immediately after. She had wept through much of the hearing, she couldn't help herself. I said it was okay, it was understandable. She said that the board members seemed kind and friendly. She said she answered all their questions and managed to say what she felt she needed to say for herself. A couple of the board members had wiped away a few tears themselves, she told me.

We were all so hopeful. Maybe this could happen. Maybe this could actually happen.

But it wasn't to be. On Christmas Eve, we learned that Kelly's petition had been denied.

I was devastated. I had dared to hope. I had also raised Kelly's hopes: She had appeared before the clemency board, her lawyers had met with the governor's counsel, and her case had finally made it to the governor's desk. We had both started to picture her walking free.

Sara tried to look at the bright side. She said, "We almost did it, we came really close." In fact, the parole officer at Bedford Hills Prison and the parole office in Peekskill had been told by higher-ups that Kelly would be getting out. The Peekskill parole officer had come to the convent to confirm where Kelly would be living. Sister Antonia was told it was going to happen and began to prepare Kelly's room.

Sara pointed out that several members of the clemency board were also on the parole board. She believed that Kelly had done well before the clemency board and would be remembered. She thought we had paved the way for Kelly to receive parole at her first eligibility in June 2005.

I was not comforted. What Sara was saying made sense, but this had been *our time*. We had worked so hard and everything had lined up so well. The legal aid board member had even talked to the governor directly. Though clemency wasn't exactly the vindication Kelly sought, it was the next best thing. What had gone wrong?

It turned out that only one living person received executive clemency from Governor Pataki in 2003: a Nigerian national with no prior record who had spent 11 years in prison for being an un- witting drug mule. His sentence was commuted. The only other person to whom the governor extended clemency that year was Lenny Bruce, who died in 1966. He received a posthumous pardon for a 40-year-old obscenity conviction.

I was happy for the commuted Nigerian but sickened by the Bruce pardon. I was sure that if Lenny Bruce had known about this, he wouldn't have been happy. He would have said, "No, not me. I don't need this. *Give it to Kelly.*" With the thousands of pris- oners in New York, it seemed a cruel joke that only dead Lenny Bruce and one Nigerian merited clemency.

Because it was Christmas, I couldn't arrange to talk to Kelly. But I didn't want her to be alone in this. So I sent a telegram. The telegram read: I'M SO SORRY. I'M NOT GIVING UP. WE'RE IN THIS TOGETHER.

When I finally talked to Kelly in a couple of days, she com- forted *me*. She said she had been worried about me, about how I would take the denial. She said she had prepared herself for bad news, but she didn't think that I had. She felt good about all we had accomplished. She thanked me for everything I had done and later wrote, "I'm very grateful to God for a friend like you, Abbe. . . . Don't worry about trying to get me out. When the time comes God will open the door."

Oh no, not God again. Where was this God anyway? As far as I was concerned, God was nowhere in sight. It was just me and Kelly.

Boundaries are a tricky thing in lawyering. The more the lawyer cares about a client the trickier they become. This is so whether the client is factually innocent or not. The length of the lawyer-client relationship also affects the way boundaries are managed.

I have been a proponent of clear-cut, unambiguous professional boundaries since my earliest days as a public defender. This has not changed over time. For me, the bottom line on boundaries—in both life and law—is captured by a Wendy Wasserstein story. While in graduate school, Wasserstein's mother took her shopping. Wasserstein was on the zaftig side and favored loose-fitting clothing and oversized shirts. Her daintier mother had other ideas. Marooned in an Ann Taylor dressing room, Wasserstein found herself trying on hanger after hanger of ill-fitting, pastel-colored garments. Every item her mother handed her emphasized the generosity of her proportions. Then her mother handed her a tiny pink linen suit. The suit was not only way too small but would have looked awful on Wasserstein no matter what size. Finally Wasserstein had had it. She grabbed her mother's hand and placed it on her own arm, and then placed it back on her mother's arm. She said to her mother, "This is me and this is you" as she moved her mother's hand back and forth, back and forth. She said, "There is a separation between us. We are not the same. If you want a pink linen suit, buy yourself a goddamn pink linen suit."[4]

I use this story (which resonates, I hope, beyond Jewish mothers and daughters) with students and young lawyers to emphasize that no matter how connected we may feel to clients, there is a clear separation between clients and lawyers, a necessary separation.⁵ We are not our clients. I love the physicality of Wasserstein's story, her moving her mother's hand back and forth. It's a perfect image. The message is unmistakable and memorable, a mantra for all relationships: "This is *me* and this is *you*."

Although I had no trouble keeping Kelly and me physically separate, it was hard not to project my own feelings on her, not to make assumptions about how she was feeling. I had to remind myself that we were different people emotionally. Putting myself in her shoes was not helpful. She had her own shoes.

It was good that Kelly was respectful of boundaries. She respected the fact that I had other clients, that there were other demands on my time, that my attention was sometimes directed elsewhere. She respected the family I had built and seemed nearly as thrilled as I was when my son, Joe, was born in 1995.

I couldn't imagine being Kelly. What would have been most crushing to me—spending my life behind bars for something I didn't do—Kelly was managing to endure. I confess that what seemed to upset Kelly most—the ordinary indignities of prison life—often seemed trivial to me. It took me a while to realize that I was focused on getting her *out* while she was coping with being *in*. She had to live there. She had to deal with her powerlessness in the most authoritarian setting. She had to cope with random, often ridiculous rules. She had to deal with the personalities, the pettiness, the posturing. She wasn't "doing time" in some abstract way. This was her life.

It killed me that this was her life.

I found myself constantly renegotiating boundaries. It wasn't that there were no boundaries, but they were different from my usual boundaries with clients. The relationship was different from my usual relationships with clients.

I acted with Kelly in ways I never acted with other clients. Contrary to my usual well-organized, efficient, to-the-point client meetings, my visits with Kelly were long and chatty and expansive. It wasn't that we got nothing done—our visits were often very productive—but sometimes the point of the visits was just to *visit*. I would catch Kelly up on developments in her case, but mostly we talked about friends and family and life. My visits were not entirely unbounded because time was limited, but they were long enough to require frequent trips to the vending machines and an occasional photo session (in the approved manner of the prison visiting room, paid for in advance by the visitor, taken by an assigned prisoner with a prison-owned Polaroid).

I did things for Kelly that I didn't ordinarily do for other clients. I intervened in prison matters (disputes with corrections officers and other inmates, problems at work, health concerns, and housing arrangements) and family matters (a dispute over her father's will and related financial matters), things I generally left to others better suited. I sent things to Kelly that went well beyond the law-related books I occasionally sent to other clients: clothes, shoes, and a variety of personal items. I sent her lesbian fiction, southern fiction, Catholic fiction (well, Mary Gordon), a Scrabble set, a portable stereo. These seemed like small things to me, the least I could do. Still, I had never done this for any other client.

There have been other clients for whom I have done unusual things. Probably the most unusual thing I ever did as a lawyer was attend family therapy sessions with the 11-year-old son of an imprisoned client. The client, who had killed her son's father, was about to be paroled. She was looking forward to being reunited with her son, whom she had not seen in several years. She couldn't wait to make up for the lost time. The boy was wary. Since his mother's incarceration, he had been living with an aunt who was unrestrained in her dislike for the boy's mother. The boy had never had any counseling about the death of his father, the incarceration of his mother, or the violence he had witnessed regularly at a young age. As time went by, he no longer knew what to think about his mother. He told his aunt—and later the therapist and me—that he was afraid she might kill *him*. I was to be a stand-in for the mother in the therapy sessions.

The sessions went well. Eventually I was allowed to take the boy to see his mother at the prison. I did so a handful of times: part lawyer, part taxi service, part chaperone. My client was grateful. She and her son worked hard to rebuild their relationship and made a home together after her release.

Occasionally I buy lunch for clients. I have been known to give elderly or disabled clients cab fare. On a handful of occasions I have escorted clients to drug or alcohol treatment, counseling centers, and hospital emergency rooms. Once or twice I have picked clients up from jail and taken them home. Yet having clients in my car can feel intimate. I become self-conscious. Can I play music? How loud? Do I have to make conversation, or can I drive in silence? If transporting clients is necessary, I prefer to have an investigator do so.

I confess to having played competitive Ping-Pong with a few juvenile clients—I can't resist a Ping-Pong paddle and a teen willing to take me on. This also felt oddly intimate.

I do not do these kinds of things all the time or for every client. When I do, I remain keenly aware of my professional role and do not depart from it. I am simply doing a bit more.

But with Kelly, I shared my own life in a way I had never done with another client. She was grateful for this in a way I never expected. When I sent her a couple of photographs of Sally and Joe in 1999, I received an exuberant thank-you note: "Received my treasured pictures of Joe and Sally. They are just wonderful. . . . Thank you for caring enough about me to share your family with me." Because this gesture meant so much to Kelly, I included her in our holiday photo mailing list from that time on. She was always so pleased to receive the photo.

As she says about her prison friends, Kelly often says that she and I have grown up together. We have known each other for so long. When I fret about getting older and note the lines on my face, she tells me I look great, better than I looked when we first met. I thank her for that. I tell her she's the one who has remained youthful, and I point to her still-flawless, peaches-and-cream complexion. I have the audacity to tell Kelly, "Here is the silver lining to these years of incarceration: Your skin has absolutely no sun damage." She has the grace to laugh.

Kelly showed me that sometimes—not often, but sometimes—being a good lawyer also means being a good friend, no matter how uncomfortable I am with the idea.

A few years ago, Calvin Trillin wrote a piece in *The New Yorker* about an avowedly innocent death row inmate named Paris Carriger, who had an unusual relationship with four women, one of them a law professor. The women, whom Carriger had gotten to know through prison correspondence, had essentially become his family. They were also the main support system in his struggle for vindication. When Carriger would call from the prison, other members of the women's families would say hello and chat for a while, as if he were an out-of-state brother or cousin.[6] Although Kelly never called me at home—I am firm about maintaining one private sphere—my own family saw Kelly as an extended family member.

When Joe was six and we were driving from Washington, D.C., to the Massachusetts coast for summer vacation, we stopped at Bedford Hills. Kelly was excited when I suggested we might pay her a visit, and Sally was equally enthusiastic. We decided that Joe, who was sturdy and sociable, could handle it. He had heard about Kelly, and was already telling people with pride that one of his moms was a lawyer who "gets people out of jail."

This is what passes for a road trip diversion for the child of a criminal defense lawyer: a prison visit. Other kids get Dairy Queen.

The visit was pleasant and uneventful, but it was meaningful to Kelly. She had never met Sally before and liked her immediately. She was delighted to meet Joe. In what was then 24 years of incarceration, my Joe was the only child who had ever visited her. He was most interested in the vending machines, and could not make enough runs for candy and soda. He seemed oblivious to the fact that we were in a prison until visiting hours were over and he saw some kids and their moms weeping.

While I was supervising Joe at the vending machines, Kelly confided to Sally that she was gay but hadn't been intimate with anyone in years. She told Sally she had had a couple of relationships early in her incarceration (something Kelly had shared with me long before) but wouldn't do it anymore because of HIV and other diseases. She said it wasn't safe. Sally was sympathetic.

I had never brought my family to meet a client before, and I expect I never will again.

I recognize that I have gotten as much out of the relationship as Kelly has, maybe more. I couldn't ask for a better friend. When she was in prison, she was my most faithful correspondent. She has remained an excellent correspondent on the outside as well. Kelly is a devoted letter writer in a world of e-mail and cell phones. Not a birthday or holiday goes by without a card from her. I don't think I ever received a Passover card from anyone else. She signs the Jewish holiday cards "Shalom."

There was a level of intensity to my relationship with Kelly that I didn't feel with other clients. It was not just that she was innocent. With her, I no longer had the safety of a strictly bounded professional role. We meant too much to each other. We created different boundaries; we reconceptualized professional role. It was unfamiliar, risky. She signed her letters "love." Soon I signed mine the same way.

Perhaps the intensity was born of tragedy. Kelly's lengthy incarceration in the face of her long-maintained innocence was so tragic it challenged all my usual methods of maintaining distance. In most cases, there is something that naturally separates me from my client, something that creates needed space. Sometimes it is the notion of professional role: I say to myself, *I am my client's lawyer, not my client's friend, sister, mother.* Sometimes it is my awareness of the client's different life circumstances and choices: I say to myself, *I did not give birth to my client, I am not responsible for how he or she came to need my services, there is only so much I can do now, shit happens.* Although I believe that "choice" lies on a spectrum—some people have more choices in life, and some have fewer—I take comfort in knowing that my clients have some individual agency. And this lifts responsibility from my shoulders.

I also couldn't make use of my usual distancing device—that Kelly had made her choices and was simply experiencing the consequences. She didn't make any choices, except choosing to take a trip north with someone she didn't know very well when she was very young. No matter how many clients for whom I have made this argument, Kelly was a true victim of circumstance.

Most bad decisions don't lead to such dire consequences. Most of us take for granted that you can make a wrong choice and get a second chance. But Kelly never got a second chance.

Kelly's cruel and needless punishment—her endless confinement as time marched on—also challenged my ability to live with a certain level of injustice. Injustice is a part of the day-to-day world of criminal practice: Criminal defenders and our clients routinely encounter arbitrariness, ignorance, and meanness by those in positions of authority. There is often no rhyme or reason to how things work. Sometimes the most sympathetic clients fare worse than the most disagreeable ones. Often the whole system seems out of whack. It's a painful realization you learn to live with. With Kelly, I couldn't live with it.

I was carrying Kelly around with me constantly. I found myself feeling guilty whenever I went to a record store, a bookstore, a movie. I was worried about her, plagued by her case, guilty about not doing enough.

I recognized that no matter how much I resisted the idea, I couldn't help but want to save Kelly, to give her back her life, to right the terrible wrong that had been done to her. This is what I was trained for, why I became a criminal lawyer. I thought about what it would have been like to represent Kelly at trial. I believed the result might have been different: The case was so triable, the identification testimony so weak, I believed I could have won it. I was probably getting carried away with myself—identification cases are notoriously tough, and Scholl had not done a bad job—but I would have given anything to have had a shot at that trial.

I was mad sometimes, both on Kelly's behalf and on my own: mad at Kelly's trial lawyer, mad at the jurors, mad at my beloved teacher Claudia, mad at the governor, mad at the *system*. Why couldn't Scholl have been more skilled? Why did he agree to try a murder case for someone with no record and a strong claim of innocence when he had never before tried a run-of-the-mill homicide? What were the jurors thinking if they were thinking at all? Did they not understand that the sole eyewitness had told the police shortly after the crime that he did not see the face of the alleged accomplice? What the hell had Claudia been doing when Kelly was offered that plea for time served? Why did she passively defer to Kelly instead of talking Kelly into pleading? Why couldn't Governor Pataki release a middle-aged woman with no record who had been locked up for 27 years on a one-witness identification case? Why couldn't the system distinguish between an innocent naïf who unsuspectingly went on a road trip with a bad guy and the bad guy himself, who unfortunately had a penchant for robbing and killing?

If everyone had done their jobs and the system had worked, Kelly would have been out years ago and I wouldn't be saddled with this hopeless, endless case.

It was hard to stay mad at Claudia, who was her own harshest critic. She was scarred from her experience representing Kelly and believed she would never get over it. She kept telling me how grateful she was that I took Kelly's case off her hands. She said, "I could never do this again, ever. I could never represent anyone who is innocent." She didn't know how I did what I did for a living.

Claudia's comment reminded me of something a friend who is a civil poverty lawyer once said during a conversation about the difference between criminal and civil work. My friend is every bit as strong an advocate for his clients as I am for mine. Still, he acknowledged that no matter how onerous the civil case, it cannot compare to being responsible for another person's *freedom*. He told a story about a serious miscalculation he once made in a case, a mistake he had had a hard time getting over. He shuddered to think of it. "Thank God it was just money," he said.

Sometimes I was mad at Kelly. After 10 years in prison, she should have known enough to take the goddamn plea when it was offered. There were plenty of people she trusted who had urged her to take that plea: her lawyer, her family, her friends. One of Kelly's closest friends at the prison was a former New York City police officer who had been convicted of murdering a man who had sexually assaulted her, a verdict that was later overturned. She begged Kelly to take the plea and get out while she could. She told Kelly she was foolish to count on complete vindication when the point was to get *out*. But Kelly had refused to budge.

Every once in a while I would get mad at Kelly for getting herself into this mess, for not seeing through Billy Ronald, for being naive and trusting and *innocent*.

Sometimes, too, I would get mad at Kelly's need for me. I didn't like being so needed, so important to her. It wasn't that Kelly was demanding; most of the time she asked for very little. Still, I felt her need. Sometimes she had legal needs and sometimes more personal ones. The problem was I wasn't meeting her needs in either category. I wasn't making a dent.

Kelly was unusually restrained about her feelings toward the cast of characters in her case. Over the years, she ran out of anger at Billy Ronald and had little to say about him. She was mostly mad at herself for associating with him at all. As she wrote in 2002, "I feel a never-ending remorse for my choice of friendship with a person I did not really know at all."

After the 2003 denial, Kelly was no longer eligible for clemency. Under New York law, prisoners who are within 18 months of parole are not allowed to seek clemency. Parole was all Kelly had left.

Ofra worked on the film. I was convinced it would be helpful. Public pressure can make a difference in parole too. A public television documentary would have an impact.

Sara said she was willing to work on Kelly's parole application when the time came. She had experience with the parole board and had had some success with parole appeals. I told her I would be happy to have her help.

Ofra's film *The Plea* aired on June 17, 2004. It was a brilliant exploration of plea bargaining in America, an instant classic. Kelly's story was told by Claudia, who was brave and eloquent, and by me. Kelly was sincere and somber. She said she could never plead guilty to a crime she did not commit, even if it meant she would spend the rest of her life in prison. Nobody watching could doubt her innocence.

Kelly looked good too. Prior to the filming there had been a quarrel about her hair. When Ofra had last seen her, Kelly's hair was close-cropped, spiky and gelled. She thought that Kelly would look softer and more appealing on-screen with longer hair, and suggested that she let it grow. Kelly was offended. She thought Ofra was trying to make her into something she wasn't: more feminine, not so gay. She wrote me an angry letter:

> Hey, Abbe. I want you to read this letter when it is quiet, away from interruption or any kind of disturbance. Now, about my

hair. Abbe, one of the reasons I love you is because you accept me the way I am, which is gay; and you *never* made me feel like I must be expected to be something I'm not or change to be what you want me to be. When I was a young country girl named Patsy I had to wear long hair to be in school or *accepted* period. That's how it was back in those days. But Abbe, if people cannot accept me the way I am now after spending over half of my life in prison then please tell them to just forget it. . . . I look "hard"? Well, that is what it took to *survive* and I'm not ashamed of it, Abbe. And hair is not going to make me look soft. They can accept me as I am or not at all.

We spoke on the phone a couple of days later. I pointed out that Kelly's hair had been many different lengths over the years, and it had nothing to do with who she was. I told her that no one was asking her to violate her sense of self; we just wanted to tell her story in the most effective way. I wasn't sure she would come around, but in the film her hair was not so short.

Kelly got a mountain of letters as a result of *The Plea.* She received mail when it was initially broadcast in the United States and more when it was broadcast abroad, in places as far away as Australia and China. Suddenly Kelly had friends and supporters all over the world.

The governor of New York must have gotten mail after *The Plea* too. Many people told Kelly they had written to the governor. The *Frontline* Web site included an address for the governor and the New York State Parole Board.

In August 2004 Kelly was told that she was approved for the Honors Floor and would be moving in shortly. She was overjoyed when it happened. She said she almost felt like a person again. In September, Kelly's brother Eddie, who had been born again and was back in Kelly's life, came to visit from North Carolina. A few months later he brought a girlfriend whom he had met at church.

Kelly suddenly had more freedom and more family than she had had in years.

In 2005 Sara called me to talk about the parole effort. She had left the Legal Aid Society but was still interested in working on Kelly's parole application. She wanted to get Kelly out, and, because of her experience and contacts, she believed she was well positioned to make it happen. But she wanted to be clear about what she was willing to do: She would take this on, but only if she was lead counsel for purposes of parole. If our efforts failed, her work was done. She would not litigate any parole appeal.

I was taken aback. I had been counting on Sara's continued involvement, especially if there was an appeal. I had no expertise whatsoever in New York parole appeals. But Sara's requirement to be in charge threw me. Kelly had been my client for years. I had been happy to work with many other people, including Sara, Scott, and the legal aid board member, but it never occurred to me that someone else would *take over.* Did Sara not think I was able? My sense of identity felt threatened: If I wasn't Kelly's lawyer, who was I?

I had to remind myself that this wasn't about *me,* it was about Kelly. Sara was a very good lawyer, was based in New York, knew the institutional players, knew the law, and would be dogged on Kelly's behalf. It was clearly in Kelly's best interests to have Sara involved. I needed to step back so this could happen. The fact that Sara was a New York lawyer seemed especially important. Among other things, she was less than an hour from Kelly and could see her more often than I could to prepare her for her appearance before the parole board (where, again, Kelly would be on her own). She would be able to meet personally with the prison parole officer who would be in charge of Kelly's case. She would be able to do more than I.

I agreed and told Sara she could take the lead in this. I said I would tell Kelly about the arrangement and would, of course, be available to assist in any way I could. I said I'd deal with the parole appeal if it came to that.

The first thing Sara felt strongly about was that there should be no press. She thought *The Plea* was excellent, but further publicity for Kelly would be counterproductive. She thought the parole board would quietly do the right thing for Kelly, and it was best to avoid controversy.

Sara did everything right. Borrowing from the clemency petition, she assembled a smaller parole packet, which included letters from Kelly's most prominent supporters, the federal district court decision, Magistrate Judge Dolinger's letter, and the polygraph examination results. She followed up on the contacts we had made in the course of the clemency effort. She got the legal aid board member who used to work for Governor Pataki involved again. She called Paul Hatch's mother and got her to write a letter saying she didn't oppose parole. She got in touch with the Oneida County District Attorney to make sure there was no active opposition to parole. She got Elaine Lord, who had recently stepped down as superintendent of Bedford Hills, to write a letter on Kelly's behalf. This was a fabulous letter. A highly respected criminal justice official, Lord went so far as to say that she believed Kelly was innocent.

Sara worked closely with the prison parole officer and with Kelly. She also kept in close contact with me.

But there was tension. One especially bad moment had to do with a letter of support Sara asked me to write that would be part of the parole packet. I wrote a two-and-a-half-page letter, introducing myself, describing my relationship to Kelly, and listing the reasons in favor of parole. The letter was both personal (it was written in my "voice" and included a personal appeal to the members of the parole board) and lawyerly (I made what I thought were the strongest arguments for Kelly's release). When I sent it to Sara, she was inexplicably furious. She said she thought we had agreed that she was Kelly's lawyer for parole. She said my letter made it seem as if I were Kelly's lawyer and not her. I said, but I *am* Kelly's lawyer; even though you are heading up the parole effort, I haven't stopped being Kelly's lawyer. She said my letter would confuse the board. I said I didn't understand what she wanted from me.

Sara said she wanted me to write a letter telling the parole board about the unusual things I had done for Kelly over the years, including buying her personal items from places like drugstore.com. I was dumbfounded. I didn't see what any of this had to do with why Kelly should be paroled. No matter what I had bought Kelly over the years—and yes, I had become a regular shopper at drugstore.com on her behalf—I wasn't her *personal shopper.* I was her lawyer. I wasn't going to write to the parole board about buying Kelly moisturizer.

Still, I felt I had to appease Sara. There was too much at stake. Plus, I had agreed to do it her way. I proposed a compromise: If Sara would incorporate some of the points I made in my letter into her own letter, then I would leave the legal arguments to her. She said okay.

On another occasion, Sara and Scott had it out. Sara was not happy that Scott was talking to people he knew in the parole system. She was not happy with some of the things Scott was saying to Kelly. She called Scott and told him that she was in charge and didn't want him interfering. The conversation was unpleasant. I had to intervene.

Maybe some tension was to be expected, especially between Sara and me. It is characteristic of lawyers to want to be in control, to want to run things. The ego is a palpable body part in an attorney, perhaps *the* most prominent body part. But I hadn't minded when the legal aid board member made the argument to the governor's counsel. And hadn't I always said that I didn't care who got credit for Kelly's release, should that day come—I just wanted her *out?*

I kept my other feelings in check.

The parole hearing was held in the March 2005. Kelly thought she did well. It sounded that way to me too. Now we just had to wait.

On Thursday night, April 21, 2005, Sara called me on my cell phone. I was at my son's baseball practice. I could tell from her voice it was good news. She told me that Kelly's parole petition had been granted. Kelly would be getting out on her very first parole eligibility date: June 13, 2005.

"That's fantastic," I said. I thanked Sara for her excellent work, and told her I couldn't thank her enough. I said I was happy for Kelly and relieved—the alternative would have been unthinkable, a parole hearing every two years with the risk of repeated rejection. Still, I couldn't help feeling that parole was a consolation prize after the clemency denial. After all, Kelly had served her full minimum sentence: 28 years and 6 months. "I guess it's easier getting someone out on parole than through clemency," I said. I don't think Sara appreciated that comment.

However, she was getting out. Kelly was *finally getting out.*

I called Kelly's brother, Eddie, to tell him the good news. He was ecstatic. I called Claudia, Scott, Ben, Ofra, and the Arthers. I also called Sally, my parents, Sally's parents, and several friends who had been anxiously awaiting the parole board's decision. Everyone was thrilled.

 ⌒

I confess that I struggled with a feeling of anticlimax. For me, Kelly's coming release was bittersweet at best. It was hardly a great victory.

The way I saw it, an innocent person had served nearly 30 years in prison. After years and years of trying to get her out, all I had accomplished was release on parole. Release on *parole*. Guilty people—people who actually committed the crime they were convicted of—get released on parole, not innocent people. Innocent people are not supposed to be locked up in the first place, and, if they are, there should at least be some *recognition* that they are innocent. I couldn't accomplish that for Kelly, not in the courts and not through clemency. So now Kelly would be released on her scheduled date and supervised by the Department of Parole.

Then I had a painful thought: Kelly might have been released on parole if I had done *absolutely nothing*, if I had never come back into her life. I understood that most people convicted of violent crimes are not released at their first eligibility. For the longest time, Kelly had been convinced that she would never be released at her first board because of the nature of her conviction. But I wasn't sure of that. Maybe it was time. Maybe 28 and a half years was enough. The prisons were overcrowded, and no one could claim that this middle-aged woman who wanted to live out her days in a convent was a danger to society.

I tried, but I couldn't feel joyful about Kelly's release. I could barely feel anything. Kelly's release was scheduled for the exact day

I was supposed to be speaking in Montreal. I felt oddly torn. I knew I had to be there at the prison gate—for me as well as for Kelly—but I had been looking forward to this conference on legal ethics. What was my problem? This was just one more academic presentation, and *Kelly was getting out of prison.* I got a friend to take my place at the conference and made plans to be in New York.

There was a lingering melancholy that I couldn't seem to shake. I felt guilty about this—it was a character flaw, a sign of narcissism. I was unable to let go of my feeling of disappointment, disenchantment. I felt I had failed Kelly. The litany of failed efforts over the years, the time lost, the *decades* came crashing down on me.

When I shared my distress with my friend Ilene, saying I wish I could just let go of *some* of these feelings, she said, "You? You can't even let go of a bad sandwich."

I tried not to show any of this to Kelly because I didn't want her to have to comfort me. But I'm sure she knew. The other thing I tried to keep from Kelly was the growing strain between Sara and me. I suspected she knew that as well.

I understood there was a range of feelings between Sara and me: feelings of envy, resentment, rivalry, hurt. The feelings went both ways. For me, it felt like I'd been trying to open a stuck jar for years, using every ounce of determination and strength, and then Sara comes in and gets it off in a single twist—as if nothing had preceded her effort. She seemed oblivious to Kelly's and my history, neither recognizing nor respecting the groundwork I had laid in Kelly's case or our deep connection. I was also envious that this was *her* victory—it seemed she had deliberately set it up that way—not mine. Sara no doubt felt that she had worked hard on the case and had succeeded. Maybe she felt insufficiently recognized too. Maybe she was grappling with her own feelings of envy (because I had been featured in *The Plea* and she hadn't? Because I had a 25-year relationship with Kelly and her couple of years couldn't compete?). I tried to talk with her about what was going on, but she refused.

We did agree that we would not let any conflicts between us get in the way of Kelly's big day.

The weeks passed quickly. Kelly was upbeat and full of energy. For the first time in decades, she was making *plans*. She learned that the catering company at the convent had offered her a job that came with medical and dental benefits—they had even ordered uniforms for her. She would also work at the convent infirmary. Kelly was so happy about all of this.

A couple of weeks before Kelly's release date, I talked with her friend Nancy. Nancy had been visiting Kelly for some years after being introduced by a mutual friend who did prison ministry. When the friend became too ill to keep visiting, she asked Nancy if she would do it. Soon Kelly and Nancy became good friends.

Nancy told me that she had been to the prison earlier that day to get Kelly's personal belongings—the things Kelly had accumulated while in prison, the things she would take to her new life. Nancy retrieved seven small boxes.

I couldn't stop thinking about those seven boxes. They reflected three decades of Kelly's life. In nearly 30 years, everything Kelly possessed could be packed up in seven small boxes.

The contrast to my own life was frightening. While Kelly was packing her handful of boxes, I was busy collecting as many cast-off grocery and liquor store boxes as I could find before biting the bullet and buying some. I had received a Fulbright scholarship to Australia, and Sally, Joe, and I were moving to Melbourne for the coming academic year. We had to make the house ready for people who would be living there while we were away. Never had I seen so much *stuff,* it was daunting. For weeks I'd been packing up clothes and toys, clearing out shelves and drawers. The basement was quickly filling up. When had I accumulated so much? There was a time when I could put everything I owned into my Honda Civic hatchback.

But there was never a time when I could put everything I owned in seven boxes.

As the date of Kelly's release approached, I was unable to focus on anything else. I tried to work on other cases, but my heart wasn't in them. I tried to get things ready for the visiting professor who would be taking over during my absence, but my heart wasn't in that either.

The only thing I was able to do with any sort of purpose was shop. I mean, really *shop.*

I poured myself into shopping, as only an obsessive can. First, I shopped for Kelly. I had already bought "parole clothes" for her: a pair of blue jeans, a bright peach colored T-shirt with a matching oversized oxford shirt. She was pleased with the whole ensemble, especially the jeans, which fit her perfectly. So I bought her another pair in black. I got her a wallet and some extra T-shirts. Next, I shopped for Joe. His camp trunk was being picked up the same morning that Sally and I were heading to New York for Kelly's release, and there were a million things I needed to get. He needed extra batteries, bug spray, basketball shoes, and 16 pair of socks. (At camp and in life, you can never have too many socks.) I shopped for Sally. She needed travel stuff for our trip abroad.

I also shopped for me. I was at my most neurotic.

I coveted two different pair of sandals I'd been seeing in the stores. Should I buy them at all? Did I really need them? Maybe I should just buy one pair, but which one? I liked them both, how could I choose? Remarkably, both were on sale, one at such a good price they might as well be *free*.

I don't know how I live with myself. I need more than seven boxes for my shoes alone.

The morning before Kelly's release, Sally and I were supposed to head for New York right after we dropped Joe off at the baseball field (he would spend the night at a teammate's house) in order to meet Ofra at 5:00 P.M. for drinks. I had vowed to leave early to avoid stress: Few things are more trying than racing through a four- or five-hour drive in an attempt to make up for lost time. But Sally wanted to work out at the gym first. I was gracious about this, notwithstanding my growing anxiety about the drive, the traffic (getting from D.C. to New York is never easy), and *Kelly getting out*. I said I'd make myself useful while she did her thing, get some gas, put the luggage in the car, and gather together a sack of odds and ends for Kelly.

When Sally wasn't ready in an hour, I tried to remain calm. Thankfully, I'd built in enough time for a slight delay. But when we finally set off and were about to get on the Beltway, a good 10 minutes away, and had to turn back because Sally forgot her cell phone, my munificence was spent. I had been really looking forward to getting together with Ofra, with whom I was hoping to cultivate a friendship. If we were too late, we would lose her to an evening event. After Sally retrieved her cell phone, we set off again with new rules: no stopping at Starbucks, no stopping for food, no bathroom stops unless it was absolutely necessary, only a brief stop for gas on the New Jersey Turnpike (because the gas is cheapest there). Every traffic jam I blamed on Sally. Every long toll line was her fault. Luckily, there weren't too many delays, and I managed to drive above the speed limit a good deal of the time. When we got to Ofra's at 5:30, we were giddy with relief.

Ofra had a fabulous two-floor Upper West Side apartment, with a backyard garden. We had lively conversation and excellent wine and cheese. The time passed quickly. Suddenly we were late to dinner with friends. One lived near the prison and was putting us up for the night. This time I couldn't blame Sally. We had a delicious dinner and more good conversation, the perfect distraction.

I slept poorly that night. I dreamed that someone had let our Welsh terrier Hapus ("happy" in Welsh) off his leash, and he ran onto a highway where he was killed by a passing car. The person who had caused this terrible tragedy then tried to pass another dog off as Hapus. This new dog wasn't even a terrier. I went along with the ruse for a while, thinking I could somehow find Hapus in this other dog. But finally I said it just wouldn't work. I couldn't attach to this dog. I wanted *my dog* back.

The year before we had lost a puppy. On my watch, it had scampered away and was hit by a bus. Was this dream a remnant of that puppy tragedy, or about the perils of freedom? Was my subconscious trying to tell me that I was fearful of the change and loss that would invariably accompany Kelly's "unleashing"? Was this dream about the continuing trauma from losing my beloved puppy (even though I had since attached, mightily, to another), or losing my beloved *client?*

The day of Kelly's release now feels like a magnificent fantasy. It's still hard to believe that it actually happened. And yet aspects of that day were completely ordinary, like any other day.

Because the prison would not say exactly when Kelly would be released, we arrived at 7:30 in the morning, after picking up a couple of espressos, that day's *New York Times,* and enough bagels and doughnuts for the small crowd that would soon assemble. Ofra and her camera crew were already at the prison when we got there, as was a friend who would be taking still photographs. All of this was with Kelly's agreement. She wanted the many people who had written to her after viewing *The Plea* to see her being released. One by one, others came: Sara and a friend, Scott, two of Kelly's prison-visiting friends, Sister Antonia, and Kelly's brother and his girlfriend.

Things with Sara were tense but civil. We shook hands and I thanked her again for everything she had done. Scott and I were delighted to see each other. He had become a friend as well as an important consultant. Kelly's brother greeted me warmly and introduced me to his girlfriend. Sister Antonia, who, aside from Kelly, had been waiting longest for this day, was overjoyed. Kelly had told me that Sister Antonia, who was in her 80s, now needed a wheelchair. She got around remarkably well in a motorized one. We were waiting in small groups as close to shade as we could get because it was supposed to reach 100 degrees that day and the sun was already beating down on us.

In retrospect, the wait was relatively short. But it was fraught and suspenseful at the time. The prison officials were at their worst. The officers sent out to monitor us were bad-tempered tyrants, like so many low-level bureaucrats with a modicum of power. They were unhappy about the cameras and ordered us all off the premises. They said anyone with the press was not allowed on state property. (Hadn't these people heard of freedom of the press?) It didn't seem to matter that most of us were not members of the press. One lieutenant ordered us to move all of our cars from the prison parking lot, knowing that there was no place else to park within a half mile of the prison and one of us was in a wheelchair.

I tried to explain to the lieutenant that none of us was the press. I introduced myself as Kelly's lawyer and pointed out various friends and family. I explained that Ofra was a public television documentary filmmaker who was doing a follow-up story to one that had already aired. I said my friend with the camera was a therapist who was taking photographs for posterity, not for a newspaper or magazine. The lieutenant did not respond. He was unwilling to have a conversation. Thankfully, a female deputy superintendent arrived who was more reasonable. We struck a deal: If we complied with the off-state-property rule by congregating across the street behind a guardrail, she let us keep our cars where they were. She seemed to accept that this was a special day for Kelly and we were a small handful of people welcoming her back to the world. I told her that I'd been coming to see Kelly at the prison for nearly 25 years and this was a special day for me too.

Giving us a taste of what Kelly had put up with these past three decades, there were "enforcers" in the parking lot who threatened us with exile anytime we wandered from our designated spot to greet someone or ask a question.

Just after 9:00 A.M., the lieutenant sent word that he wanted to see Kelly's brother. Eddie walked up to the prison visitor screening room. The lieutenant offered Eddie the option of driving his car up to the prison gate to collect Kelly and take her away quietly in order to avoid the "media circus." Eddie politely declined. He told the lieutenant that his sister wanted to walk out herself and greet her friends and family. *Good for Eddie!* I thought.

Suddenly there was Kelly, aglow in the peach ensemble I had sent for this moment. Everyone could spot her. There she was: she was at the gate, the gate opened, she was walking through the gate, *she was on the other side of the gate.* Kelly was *on the other side.* She looked radiant. With the prison parole officer close at hand (a lovely man who had been helpful to Kelly—and who was crying, she said), Eddie escorted her out. It was an amazing sight. I had been dry-eyed until that moment but suddenly began to weep. Years and years of imagining this moment and believing it might never happen poured out of me. Here was Patsy Kelly Jarrett walking out of the prison, walking where she had not stepped foot for nearly 30 years, walking toward us, free.

We were kept back behind the prison property line until Kelly greeted Sister Antonia (who was allowed to remain in the parking lot because of the wheelchair) and Eddie's girlfriend, who was with the sister. Then she headed for me. We hugged long and hard while I wept in her arms. Then she hugged Sara and everyone else. The whole thing truly felt like a dream, which is what Kelly kept saying.

We all got into our cars and headed off, caravan style. We stopped a half block from the prison for more photographs and so that the Ofra and the camera guys could put a microphone on Kelly. After five minutes of freedom, they asked Kelly how she felt. She was eloquent. She said, "It all feels like a dream, but I think I feel the way the people who made it out of the World Trade Center on September 11 felt. I feel happy for myself but full of sorrow for those who didn't make it out. My thoughts and prayers are with the women who are still in prison and don't need to be there."

Sara and some of the others left right after the roadside photo shoot. I hugged her good-bye. The tension lifted and a more manageable corps of people remained.

The rest of the day flew by. We went to the convent that would be Kelly's home for the near future and possibly longer. Having never stepped foot in a convent, I was a little hesitant until Ofra, who is Israeli, declared that it was like a kibbutz. This was an inspired comparison. Kelly was joining a community. The communal dining room (a beautiful, open, sun-lit room overlooking the Hudson River) was full of cheerful bustle. The only difference was there was no resident under the age of 60, and most seemed to be in their 80s.

There was one nun who looked to be about Kelly's age, someone who was a protégée of Sister Antonia. Eddie had told me she played the guitar. This detail made me hopeful that she could be a friend for Kelly. A guitar-playing nun summoned up the image of Julie Andrews in *The Sound of Music,* Sally Field in *The Flying Nun,* or Whoopi Goldberg in *Sister Act.* Unfortunately, this nun had nothing in common with the movie nuns except for the guitar, which I never heard her play. What charm she possessed was not readily apparent. Let's just say you would not want to get on her bad side.

Immediately upon arriving at the convent, Kelly went to the chapel to pray. She wanted to thank God for her freedom. I figured she also wanted time to herself, to let her new reality set in a little.

When she emerged, we gathered around while she unpacked. The sisters had cleaned and decorated the room that was to be Kelly's, which looked like an old-fashioned college dorm room. She was to live in a wing of the convent reserved for visitors, often families of prisoners who had loved ones in nearby correctional facilities. There was a neatly tucked-in bed, a wooden bureau, and a small table. A WELCOME HOME banner hung on the door, along with photographs of Kelly's family and a tacked-up T-shirt with an American flag and the words "FREEDOM ROCKS."

It was a scene I could not have imagined. I was lounging on Kelly's bed while she unpacked—neatly folding and putting away clothes, lining up her shoes in the closet—as if we were a couple of college roommates. She opened the gifts people gave her and immediately put her "gate money" (the state gives released prisoners 40 dollars to start a new life) in her new wallet. She tried on a pair of clogs I had brought and declared them *perfect*. Scott gave her especially thoughtful gifts: a piece of luggage, a beautiful leather purse, and a special present from his wife: a small diamond-and-ruby cross.

Kelly went with Sister Antonia to meet her parole officer. I had hoped to do this with her, and had made several calls to arrange it, but the sister made it clear that she would accompany Kelly. When they returned, I took everyone (Kelly, Eddie, his girlfriend, the girlfriend's daughter and 12-year-old grandson, Sister Antonia, the guitar-playing nun, Scott, and Sally) out for a "festive lunch" in a rather prosaic seafood restaurant suggested by the sisters.

The mood was celebratory. Everyone ordered large plates of seafood and frothy, nonalcoholic drinks. There were many toasts in Kelly's honor.

I couldn't take my eyes off Kelly. She was amazing. I was astonished by her calm and self-possession. The last time I had had lunch with a woman who had just been released from prison—after "only" seven years of incarceration—my client had been a nervous wreck. She could barely order a sandwich, asking me to do it for her because she couldn't cope with the *choices*. Kelly ordered shrimp: her first seafood in 28 years.

Kelly kept saying she felt strong because God was with her and so were all of us. I think she was in a state of shock.

She kept thanking everyone: the friends and family assembled, the restaurant wait staff, God. I understood her gratitude, but at the same time I wished she didn't have to be so goddamned grateful. Would she always be so servile and submissive, or would she one day throw off this vestige of prison life? It's a terrible thing to be so helpless and grateful.

Still, I was enthralled with the sight of Kelly in the world, Kelly in a restaurant, Kelly in my car. I liked seeing her with her brother (a sweet guy, if a little too full of banter—probably he was overwhelmed). I liked seeing her out among us. But I was also aware of a jumble of feelings that didn't quite fit the celebratory mood. I was happy and relieved for Kelly. I was glad she had family, makeshift though it seemed. I couldn't help feeling sad about all the time she served and angry, angry, *angry* about her wasted youth. Where does one go with this kind of anger? Sister Antonia talked about how this was "God's plan," that Kelly had "touched so many lives while in prison" and that she was "never imprisoned in her soul." I said, "What a lovely way to look at it," when I really wanted to scream, *What are you, crazy? Kelly was so imprisoned, they stole nearly everything from her, she would have touched as many lives on the outside, God's will my ass.* But I held my tongue.

Sister Antonia was especially fierce. When I foolishly reminded her that she and Kelly had both wanted to give up for a while, and stop the efforts to get her out, she shot back, "I did not give up, I just had no faith in the *system.*"

Whatever.

When I dropped Kelly back at the convent and we said our good-byes, I was emotionally exhausted and full of sorrow. What was wrong with me? Here was Kelly, about to embark on life again, the long fight for freedom finally over. Yet instead of wanting to shout for joy, I felt like getting into bed and staying there. Instead of basking in the glow of a remarkable release, redemption, *rebirth,* I felt like someone had died.

It was partly the convent. No matter how perfect it was for Kelly in the short term, it felt confining. It was a cosseted, protected, small life. I wanted Kelly to *live* again. I wanted her to spread her wings. I wanted her to have friends and family and adventure and maybe even a little *romance*. Although she could never really "make up for lost time," I wanted her to give it a shot. When I told Sister Antonia that I was worried that Kelly was talking about joining the convent and not just living there, she reassured me. She said that Kelly was in no position to think about such a thing, she had her hands full getting used to being free. She said she had made it clear to Kelly that Kelly didn't owe her anything—she would love Kelly no matter what she did with her life—and she didn't owe the convent anything either. She also said that the convent would not allow Kelly to declare any sort of intention until she knew who she was in the world.

I almost said *Thank God.*

But it was more than the convent. I had to admit that my feeling of sorrow was connected to a feeling of deep loss. But what was this about?

My friend Ilene again provided wisdom. She suggested that I had been on this mission to free Kelly for a quarter century, and the end of all that—Kelly finally getting out—was bound to be difficult. She pointed out that Kelly had been a big part of my professional identity and more: She had been my *life's work*. She said it reminded her of her search for the perfect black linen blazer. She has been looking for one for more than 10 years. If she ever finds it, she will have no purpose in life.

It's good to have a friend who understands me so well.

Ilene also observed that the quality in me that allowed me to attach as deeply as I did to Kelly—and to sustain the attachment for so many years—is what makes the separation and changed role so hard. It's all of a piece, she said.

Though I would never have wanted it any other way, I had to acknowledge that I was feeling the loss of Kelly as a client.

It was probably good that I lived a distance away. Had I been closer, I would have been tempted to be with Kelly a lot, probably too much, those first few days. I had this deeply maternal fantasy of holding her while she slept so that she wouldn't wake up alone those first few days. I felt the loss of her parents—as I'm sure she did—sharply. It was helpful that Sister Antonia, whom Kelly called "Mother," was close at hand. But it wasn't enough.

What I really wanted for Kelly was a partner to love her and hold her, someone who would let her cry and make her laugh. Not a bunch of elderly nuns. I felt lonely for Kelly, lonely and scared. I guess I felt lonely and scared for me too.

But still, at last, Patsy Kelly Jarrett was free.

Epilogue

Kelly has been free for more than three years now. She continues to live at the Mount Saint Frances Convent, but has moved to a one-bedroom apartment on the grounds. After obtaining a nurse's aide license, she now works two jobs: caring for sick and elderly nuns in the convent infirmary and providing in-home nursing care in and around Peekskill. She also volunteers one morning a week at a homeless shelter

She has a bank account, credit card, and cell phone. She got her driver's license and, with help from a friend, bought a car. She uses the car for work but not much else. She stays close to the convent when she's not working.

To no one's surprise, Kelly has done well on parole, and her parole officer is full of praise. She routinely tells Kelly that she wishes all of her clients were like her. Kelly is nothing if not conscientious. She complies with every rule of parole, has never missed a meeting, and regularly pays her monthly thirty-dollar parole fee. Because she is a model parolee, she does not have to report in person as often anymore.

Also, to no one's surprise, Kelly has had absolutely no trouble with the law.

Kelly has friends with whom she occasionally goes to the gym or to a movie. One or two are under 70. She remains in close touch with her brother, Eddie, who separated from his girlfriend. She spends most of her time working.

With her parole officer's permission, Kelly spent her first post-release Thanksgiving with Eddie and her old friend Terry in North Carolina. It was a memorable time. Kelly had never been on a plane before. She flew to Raleigh-Durham in a window seat, looking down on the clouds. She hadn't felt that free in a long time.

In North Carolina, she rode a horse for the first time in decades. She got on and was soon galloping. It was as if she had never stopped riding.

It was both hard and easy for Kelly to be back home. The hardest part was her father's absence and especially visiting his grave. The easiest part was being with friends and family. Though Kelly noted the many changes that had taken place while she was away— a highway ran through what used to be an open field, strip malls and housing developments were everywhere, many of the old buildings had been torn down, including her father's store—it also felt to her that she had never left. She said it was like a movie that had been made without her, and now she was back in the sequel.

She was pleased that her father's house was still standing.

I am so proud of everything Kelly has accomplished since her release. She has made a remarkable adjustment. It wasn't easy rejoining the world after such a long absence, and there have been many frustrations and obstacles. But Kelly managed to navigate her way through them all.

I remain worried about Kelly's social isolation and her unwillingness to make new friends. She is too frightened to join any clubs or pursue a hobby where she might meet people. She doesn't trust her judgment in friends. Her choice of a friend back in her youth cost her 28 years of her life, and she says she will not make that mistake again. She says she has all the friends she needs. I can't seem to persuade her otherwise.

When I suggest contacting a local gay and lesbian organization and maybe getting involved in some volunteer work there as a way of meeting people, she is dismissive. She says she doesn't want to hang out with a bunch of hard-drinking, partying lesbians. When I say that I had in mind some hardworking, middle-aged lesbians—women who would be more into Pilates than partying in their limited spare time—she says she has enough friends for now.

She says she does not want to be in a romantic relationship. She was bossed around enough in prison and doesn't need anyone else bossing her around.

Since Kelly's release, I have become increasingly aware of our differences. When the movie *Brokeback Mountain* came out, I urged Kelly to see it. This was amazing, to be able to say to Kelly I just saw a great movie and you should run out and see it. I had found the original Annie Proulx short story moving, and the film equally so. I thought it might resonate for Kelly because it was a story about forbidden gay love in rural, small-town America. Kelly went to see it with a church friend and her response was tepid. "Didn't you like it?" I asked. "Well, it was awfully explicit and my friend wondered if I was trying to convert her or something," she said. "But what did you think of it?" I asked. "It was okay," she said. "Didn't you feel for the two men who weren't allowed to love each other openly?" I asked. "Well," she said. "To tell you the truth, I felt sorrier for the wife whose husband was cheating on her. I think if you're gay you should just be gay and not get married and cheat on someone."

What made me think we would feel the same way? Did I *need* us to feel the same way? Why was I surprised by Kelly's reaction? Again Wendy Wasserstein's injunction echoed in my mind: *This is me and this is you and this is me.*

Thank goodness Kelly has the freedom to feel however she wants about *Brokeback Mountain*.

On the anniversary of Kelly's first year of freedom, I bought her a ring. It is sterling silver and has an inscription. On the outside it says: "If you have faith . . ." and on the inside "anything is possible."

Kelly said it was absolutely perfect.

She is wearing it next to her Jesus ring.

As I look back on the years that I have known Kelly, and the years of trying to free her, I am aware of the toll the struggle has taken. Although I am happy that Kelly is among us, I am sad about how long it took to get her out. I hate the fact that she is under the supervision of the parole system. I also hate it that she remains so frightened that she keeps largely to herself. It feels like a broken life, and I couldn't manage to fix that.

Maybe this is unfair to Kelly, the suggestion that her life is broken. And maybe it is too soon to tell. Knowing Kelly, she'll figure things out for herself.

Representing Kelly has been an honor. It is surely my case of a lifetime.

But as a criminal defense lawyer, I need to say again that defending the innocent is no more virtuous than defending the guilty. Kelly happened to be innocent, and her innocence raised special challenges. But I would have represented her with passion and purpose even if she had been in the car that day. Criminal defenders represent the guilty and innocent alike. We act for people in trouble. As one longtime defender puts it, "There is good in the worst of us and bad in the best of us."[1] As another says, "Each of us is more than the worst thing we ever did."[2] There is a fundamental human dignity in everyone,[3] and it is the calling of defenders to protect it.

Still, defending the innocent is an extraordinary burden. It is constant and unrelenting. It is both a professional burden and a deeply personal one.

Representing Kelly posed a challenge to everything I believe in, including myself. When I went to law school, I thought the criminal justice system was essentially fair. I saw that poor people and minorities bore the brunt of it, but I felt sure that if everyone did their job properly—police, lawyers, judges—no terrible injustice would occur. I knew that the system wasn't perfect and there were real challenges for lawyers representing the poor, but I thought it was possible to make a difference.

I had no idea how utterly random justice could be. I had no idea how routine the injustice.

I believed that I was particularly well suited to the work. I was committed, determined, impassioned. I was the product of an elite education. I had been well trained in criminal defense both at law school and in an excellent public defender's office. I had been told that I was talented. All this made me feel that I had the power to make a difference.

I was naive.

The assumption that the system works and that those who are caught up in it are guilty is pervasive. It is hard enough to fight that assumption prior to trial when the accused is supposed to be presumed innocent. Once there is a conviction, the system doubles back on itself, becoming impenetrable. The legal niceties have been applied. The jury has spoken. Only under extraordinary circumstances will a verdict be undone.

Kelly wanted me to help her prove a negative: that she wasn't there when an awful crime was committed. I tried but couldn't do that for her. I managed to get her out but not on her terms. There is no vindication. Every time she pays her parole fee she is reminded of this fact. She is told that she will be on parole for life. She will live out her days as a convicted murderer.

I have never felt so powerless as when I represented Kelly, or so discouraged. I did everything I could think of to free her. None of it worked. I talked to people in high places and low. Nobody listened. It didn't matter how articulate I was or how persuasive my cause. Nobody budged. The system was unyielding.

In more than 25 years of law practice, I have represented a handful of other clients I believed to be innocent. I have represented many clients who were not guilty of the crime charged and many more who, guilty or not, did not deserve to be so harshly punished. In all the time I have been a lawyer, I have never had another case like Kelly's. I am glad of that. I don't think I could bear another.

Acknowledgments

*I*t can't be true that writing this book was as hard as getting Kelly out. But sometimes it felt that way.

I owe many debts to many people.

Helen Garner, the great Australian writer, was the first to read the manuscript, and offered crucial guidance and encouragement throughout the writing and publishing process. Against her sage advice, I shared drafts with a few trusted friends and loved ones, who cheered me on and made (mostly) helpful suggestions: Jane Aiken, Louise Bowen, Corrine Fletcher, Sally Greenberg, Barbara Pizer, and Robin Steinberg. Then there were those who were willing to listen to me read the manuscript out loud—basically anyone who wandered into my office after hours, or who happened to be within earshot or made the mistake of phoning me while I was writing. These include: Tucker Carrington, Cecile Chapaveyre, Emily Findlay, Jane Greenberg, Joe Greenberg, Jeannie Hess, Judy Levin, Loni Smith McKown, Alyson Myers, and assorted postgraduate fellows in Georgetown's E. Barrett Prettyman Fellowship Program.

Many others expressed interest in this project and lent support in a variety of ways. Of particular note are: Bernice Blitz, Shelley Broderick, Karen Friedman, Michael Gawenda, Albert

Greenberg, Tracy Hughes, Mark Levine, Avis Murray, Joe Margulies, Suneel Nelson, John Carl Scholl, Teruko Scriven, Anna Selden, Anita Smith, David Smith, Glenn Smith, Pam Smith Stern, Audrey Snow, Karen Tokarz, Ellen Yaroshefsky, and Ben and Jake Catt. I am especially grateful to Stephanie Von Hirshberg for her early enthusiasm and advice. Dean Alex Aleinikoff of the Georgetown University Law Center provided a timely research sabbatical, allowing me an opportunity to write uninterrupted. He has been a great source of encouragement, as have Georgetown colleagues Sheryll Cashin, Deborah Epstein, Steve Goldblatt, Vicki Jackson, Emma Coleman Jordan, Carrie Menkel-Meadow, Mike Seidman, Robin West, and the late Sam Dash. I also want to thank Anthony Amsterdam, Monroe Freedman, Howard Lesnick, and Stephen Wizner, whose kind interest in my writing over the years has helped me to believe in myself.

My partner Sally once declared that I go through the five stages of grief whenever anyone edits me. She's right. Still, I am grateful to have worked with a superb editor, Luba Ostashevsky, at Palgrave Macmillan. Her good judgment has made this a better book. Likewise, I could not have completed this book without the editorial assistance of my dear friend and co-conspirator Ilene Seidman. I thank her for her intelligence, generosity, fearlessness, and ability to make me laugh no matter what.

I am also grateful to Peter Matson, my literary agent at Sterling Lord Literistic, and his assistant, Rebecca Friedman, for their wise counsel throughout the process and for finding something of value in an early draft of the manuscript. Without them I would not be in a position to be writing acknowledgments.

With regard to my work on behalf of Kelly, I want to recognize all those who stood by her over the years: students and professors from NYU, Harvard, and Georgetown law schools; two former superintendents at Bedford Hills Correctional Facility (especially Elaine Lord); former and current Bedford Hills inmates and staff; and a small handful of devoted friends and family. Kelly wouldn't have made it without these people in her corner. Then there are those whose efforts were critical to her release: Claudia Angelos, Richard Arther, Catherine Arther, Sara Bennett, Ofra Bikel, Scott Christianson, Ben Gershman, Sarah Smith, and Paul Shechtman.

I thank Kelly for sharing her life with me and for letting me write this book.

Finally, I could not have written this book, or gotten Kelly out, without the love and endless patience of Sally and Joe. I thank my lucky stars to have such a family.

Notes

Chapter 1, Innocence

1. Barbara A. Babcock, "Defending the Guilty," *Cleveland State Law Review* 32 (1983–84): 175–176.
2. John Kaplan, "Defending Guilty People," *University of Bridgeport Law Review* 7 (1986): 255.
3. George Sharswood, An *Essay on Professional Ethics* (Philadelphia: T. & J. Johnson & Co., 1884).
4. Charles Curtis, "The Ethics of Advocacy," *Stanford Law Review* 4 (1951): 13–18.
5. David McCullough, *John Adams* (New York: Simon & Schuster, 2001), 65–66.
6. Ibid., 67 (quoting Cesare de Beccaria).
7. Ibid. (quoting a letter by John Adams).
8. See John B. Mitchell, "The Ethics of the Criminal Defense Attorney—New Answers to Old Questions," *Stanford Law Review* 32 (1980): 293.
9. See Monroe H. Freedman, *Lawyers' Ethics in an Adversary System* (Indianapolis: Bobbs-Merrill, 1975).
10. James Mills, "'I Have Nothing to Do with Justice,'" *Life,* March 12, 1971, 65.
11. Frank Galbally, *Galbally for the Defence* (Ringwood, Victoria: Viking/Penguin Books Australia, 1993): 1–2.
12. Clarence Darrow, *The Story of My Life* (New York: Charles Scribner's Sons, 1934), 75–76.
13. Babcock, "Defending the Guilty," 177–179.
14. For examples of such stories in both feature films and documentaries, see: *A Lesson Before Dying* (HBO, 1999) (story of an illiterate young black man wrongly accused of participating in a robbery that turned deadly); *Capturing the Friedmans* (HBO, 2003) (documentary raising questions about the innocence of a father and son accused of child molesting); *The Fugitive* (Warner Bros. Pictures, 1993) (story of a man wrongly convicted of murdering his wife who escapes from

prison to find the true culprit); *Gideon's Trumpet* (CBS Television/ Hallmark Hall of Fame Productions, 1980) (story of Clarence Earl Gideon—the man behind the *Gideon* decision—who was wrongly accused of breaking into a pool hall); *The Green Mile* (Warner Bros. Pictures, 1999) (story of an innocent man on death row); *Innocence Lost* (PBS, 1991) (documentary about daycare providers wrongly accused of child sexual abuse in a small town in North Carolina); Murder on a Sunday Morning (HBO, 2001) (documentary about a 15-year-old African American boy wrongly accused of a 2000 murder in Jacksonville, Florida) *My Cousin Vinny* (Twentieth Century-Fox, 1992) (comedy about two New Yorkers wrongly accused of murder in the deep South and the exploits of their inexperienced lawyer); *Nuts* (Warner Bros. Pictures, 1987) (story of a high-class call girl who killed in self-defense); *Presumed Innocent* (Warner Bros. Pictures, 1990) (story of an innocent lawyer accused of murder); *Scottsboro: An American Tragedy* (PBS, 2000) (documentary about the Scottsboro case in which eight young black men were wrongly convicted of rape); *Suspect* (TriStar Pictures, 1987) (story of a public defender's efforts on behalf of an innocent homeless man); *The Thin Blue Line* (American Playhouse/Channel 4 Television, 1988) (documentary about an innocent man sentenced to death in Texas); *To Kill a Mockingbird* (Universal Pictures, 1962) (classic American story about a black man wrongly accused of raping a white woman); *True Believer* (Columbia Pictures, 1989) (story of a left-wing lawyer's defense of a wrongly accused man); *The Wrong Man* (Warner Bros. Pictures, 1956) (story of a man wrongly accused of robbery and the destructive consequences to his family).

15. J. D. Salinger, *The Catcher in the Rye* (Boston: Little, Brown, 1951), 172.
16. See Richard Moran, "The Presence of Malice," *New York Times,* August 2, 2007, A21. The exonerations in the study were from 1973 to 2007.
17. Babcock, "Defending the Guilty," 180.
18. See McCullough, *John Adams,* 68.
19. Mary Halloran, "An Ode to Criminal Lawyers," *California Lawyer* (June 1998): 96.
20. Anthony Amsterdam, *Trial Manual 5 for the Defense of Criminal Cases* (ABA/ALI: Philadelphia, 1988), 339.
21. For a discussion of the "conscientious prosecutor," see Monroe H. Freedman and Abbe Smith, *Understanding Lawyers' Ethics,* 3rd ed. (New York: Lexis/Nexis, 2004), 339–40. For a discussion of the prosecutor's ethical obligation to avoid wrongful convictions, see Bruce A. Green, "Prosecuting Means More than Locking Up Bad Guys," *Litigation* 32 (Fall 2005): 12.

22. Sean Gardiner, "For Them, No Justice; Bad Convictions Put 13 Men in Prison, Persistence—and Luck—Got Them Out," *Newsday,* December 8, 2002, A3.

23. Robin Topping, "Panel Puts Justice before Prosecution," *Newsday,* January 8, 2003, A21.

24. *North Carolina v. Alford,* 400 U.S. 25 (1970).

25. See Jean Harris, *Marking Time: Letters from Jean Harris to Shana Alexander* (New York: Charles Scribner's Sons, 1991), 142–143.

26. Ibid.,144–145.

Chapter 2, Truth

1. James Mills, " 'I Have Nothing to Do with Justice,'" *Life,* March 12, 1971, 65 (quoting Martin Erdmann).

2. James S. Kunen, *How Can You Defend Those People?: The Making of a Criminal Lawyer* (New York: Random House, 1983). 3–5.

3. *Herrera v. Collins,* 505 US 390 (1993).

4. Barry Winston, "Stranger than True: Why I Defend Guilty Clients," *Harpers* (December 1986): 70.

5. Janet Malcolm, *The Trial of Sheila McGough* (New York: Alfred A. Knopf, 1999), 26.

6. R. C. L. Lindsay, "Expectations of Eyewitness Performance: Jurors' Verdicts Do Not Follow from Their Beliefs," in *Adult Eyewitness Testimony: Current Trends and Developments,* ed. David Frank Ross, J. Don Reid, and Michael P. Toglia, 362 (Cambridge: Cambridge University Press, 1994); see also Arye Rattner, "Convicted but Innocent: Wrongful Conviction and the Criminal Justice System," *Law and Human Behavior* 12 (1988): 289–292.

7. *US v. Wade,* 388 U.S. 218, 228 (1967). Justice Thurgood Marshall voiced the same concern in *Manson v. Brathwaite,* 432 U.S. 98, 119–120 (1977) (J. Marshall, dissenting) (referring to the "unusual threat to the truth-seeking process posed by the frequent untrustworthiness of eyewitness identification testimony" which "[j]uries seem . . .not inclined to discredit").

8. Glanville Llewellyn Williams, *The Proof of Guilt: A Study of the English Criminal Trial* (London: Stevens and Sons, 1955),106.

9. See http://innocenceproject.org, last visited February 28, 2008 (reporting 213 exonerations as of that date).

10. Gary L. Wells, "Eyewitness Identification Evidence: Science and Reform," *The Champion* 29 (2005): 12; James M. Doyle, "Two Stories of Eyewitness Error," *The Champion* 27 (2003): 24; Jim Dwyer, Barry

Scheck, and Peter Neufeld, *Actual Innocence* (New York: Doubleday, 2000).

11. Hugo Munsterberg, *On the Witness Stand: Essays on Psychology and Crime* (New York: Doubleday, Page & Co., 1909).

12. Edwin Borchard, *Convicting the Innocent: Errors of Criminal Justice* (1932) (Cambridge, MA: Da Capo Press, 1970).

13. Jennifer Thompson, "I Was Certain, but I Was Wrong," *New York Times,* June 18, 2000, D4, 15.

14. *Cotton v. North Carolina,* 394 S.E. 456 (N.C. App. 1990).

15. Thompson, "I Was Certain, but I was Wrong."

16. Michael R. Leippe, "The Appraisal of Eyewitness Testimony," in Ross et al., eds., *Adult Eyewitness Testimony,* 385.

17. Elizabeth F. Loftus, *Eyewitness Testimony* (Cambridge, MA: Harvard University Press, 1979), 9.

18. *Kampshoff v. Smith,* 698 F.2d 581, 585 (2d Cir. 1983) (citations and footnote omitted). See also *Jackson v. Fogg,* 589 F.2d 108, 112 (2d Cir. 1978) (calling identification testimony the "least reliable . . .[o]f all the various kinds of evidence").

19. Timothy P. O'Toole, "District of Columbia Public Defender Survey: What Do Jurors Understand about Eyewitness Reliability? Survey Says . . .," *The Champion* 29 (April 2005): 28; see also www.nlada.org /Defender/forensics; http://www.pdsdc.org/SpecialLitigation/index .asp.

20. Elizabeth F. Loftus, "Ten Years in the Life of an Expert Witness," *Law & Human Behavior* 10 (1986): 246.

21. Ibid., 250, n. 3; see also C. A. Elizabeth Luus and Gary L. Wells, "Eyewitness Identification Confidence," in Ross et al., eds., *Adult Eyewitness Testimony,* 348; Brian L. Cutler, Steven Penrod, and T. K. Martens, "The Reliability of Eyewitness Identification," *Law and Human Behavior* 11 (1987): 234 ; Kenneth A. Deffenbacher, "Eyewitness Accuracy and Confidence," *Law and Human Behavior* 4 (1980): 258.

22. See Michael R. Leippe, "The Case for Expert Testimony about Eyewitness Memory," *Psychology, Public Policy and Law* 1 (1995): 909 (discussing the importance of expert testimony on eyewitness testimony and urging the psychological and legal professions to develop responsible guidelines for use of expert testimony in court).

23. Loftus, *Eyewitness Testimony,* 55.

24. Gary L. Wells et al., "Eyewitness Identification Procedures: Recommendations for Lineups and Photospreads," *Law and Human Behavior* 22 (1998): 603.

25. Ibid., 581, 596.

26. National Institute of Justice, *A Guide for Law Enforcement* (Washington, DC: U.S. Department of Justice, Office of Justice Programs, 1999).

27. Bill Nettles, Zoe Sanders Nettles, and Gary L. Wells, "Eyewitness Identification: 'I Noticed You Paused on Number Three,'" *The Champion* 20 (November 1996): 10–11; see also Gary L. Wells, "Police Lineups as Experiments: Social Methodology as a Framework for Properly Conducted Lineups," *Personality and Social Psychology Bulletin* 16 (1990): 106–117.

28. Gary L. Wells, "Psychology of Lineups," *Journal of Applied Social Psychology* 14 (1984): 89–103; Gary L. Wells et al., "Recommendations for Properly Conducted Lineup Identification Tasks," in Ross et al., eds., *Adult Eyewitness Testimony,* 223–244.

29. David L. Feige, "I'll Never Forget That Face: The Science and Law of the Double-Blind Sequential Lineup," *The Champion* 26 (2002): 28.

30. Kate Zernike, "Study Fuels Debate over Police Lineups," *New York Times,* April 19, 2006, A1.

31. Ibid. For a helpful discussion of recent studies on lineup structure and implementation, see Beth Schuster, "Police Lineups: Making Eyewitness Identification More Reliable," *National Institutes of Justice Journal* 258 (October 2007), available at http://www.ojp.usdoj.gov/nij/journals/288/police-lineups.html.

32. Patrik Jonsson, "The police lineup is becoming suspect practice," *Christian Science Monitor,* February 6, 2007, 1; Amy Klobuchar and Hilary Lindell Califiuri, "Protecting the Innocent/Convicting the Guilty: Hennepin County's Pilot Project in Blind Sequential Eyewitness Identification," *William Mitchell Law Review* 32 (2005): 15–16. For a detailed discussion of the Hennepin County, Minnesota, pilot project in blind sequential eyewitness identification, see ibid., 17–26.

33. Jonsson, "The police lineup is becoming suspect practice," 1; Klobuchar and Califiuri, "Protecting the Innocent/Convicting the Guilty," 15–16; Amanda Paulson and Sara Miller Llana, "In police lineups, is the method the suspect?" *Christian Science Monitor,* April 24, 2006, 1. For an up-to-date report on eyewitness identification reform in state legislatures, see http://www.nacdl.org/sl_docs.nsf/Issues/eyewitnessid?OpenDocument, last visited February 28, 2008.

34. Feige, "I'll Never Forget That Face," 28; Schuster, "Police Lineups: Making Eyewitness Identification More Reliable," 2–5; U.S. Department of Justice, Office of Justice Programs, National Institute of Justice, *Eyewitness Evidence: A Guide for law Enforcement* (October 1999), 29–38 (offering protocols for both simultaneous and sequential identification procedures),.

35. *National Jury Project, Jurywork: Systematic Techniques,* 2nd ed. (1983) (Eagan, MN: Thomson/West, 2005).
36. Robert O'Harrow Jr., "From Behind Bars, Ring Collects Va. Tax Refunds," *Washington Post,* January 23, 1992, B1.
37. W. H. Auden, "September 13, 1931."
38. Bruce Springsteen, "Nebraska" (from the album *Nebraska,* 1982).

Chapter 3, Hope

1. A popular text on client interviewing is David A. Binder et al., *Lawyers as Counselors: A Client-Centered Approach,* 2nd ed. (Eagan, MN: Thomson/West, 2004). I read an earlier incarnation of this book in law school. David A. Binder and Susan C. Price, *Legal Interviewing and Counseling: A Client-Centered Approach* (St. Paul, MN: West Publishing Co., 1977). Another influential book offering a similar (though more eclectic) approach is Gary Bellow and Bea Moulton, *The Lawyering Process: Materials for Clinical Instruction in Advocacy* (Mineola, NY: The Foundation Press, 1978).
2. *Commonwealth v. Carr,* 580 A.2d 1362 (Pa. Super. Ct. 1990); see also Claudia Brenner and Hannah Ashley, *Eight Bullets: One Woman's Story of Surviving Anti-Gay Violence* (Ithaca, NY: Firebrand Books, 1995); H. L. Pohlman, *The Whole Truth? A Case of Murder on the Appalachian Trail* (Amherst: University of Massachusetts Press, 1999); Abbe Smith, "On Representing a Victim of Crime," in *Law Stories: Law, Meaning, and Violence,* ed. Gary Bellow and Martha Minow (Ann Arbor: University of Michigan Press, 1996). 149–167.
3. Barbara A. Babcock, "Defending the Guilty," *Cleveland State Law Review* 32 (1983–84): 177–179.
4. Ibid., 178–179.
5. Ibid., 175.
6. Siobhan Roth, "Attorneys Shy Away from Defending Terror Suspects," *The Recorder,* December 3, 2001, 3; "A Nation Challenged; Prosecutors Detail Case," *New York Times,* November 27, 2001, B7.
7. Brooke A. Masters, "Va. Case a Window on Terror Probe," *Washington Post,* November 29, 2001, A20.
8. William J. Brennan, Jr., "What the Constitution Requires," *New York Times,* April 28, 1996, D13.
9. Charles J. Ogletree, Jr., "Beyond Justifications: Seeking Motivations to Sustain Public Defenders," *Harvard Law Review* 106 (1993): 1239.
10. Ibid., 1272. For an essay arguing that the moral foundation of the lawyer-client relationship is friendship, see Charles Fried, "The

Lawyer as Friend: The Moral Foundations of the Lawyer-Client Relation," *Yale Law Journal* 85 (1976): 1060.

11. Ogletree, "Beyond Justifications," 1275.

12. Abbe Smith, "Too Much Heart and Not Enough Heat: The Short Life and Fractured Ego of the Empathic, Heroic Public Defender," *University of California at Davis Law Review* 37 (2004): 1243–1264.

13. Anthony Amsterdam, *Trial Manual V For the Defense of Criminal Cases* (Philadelphia: ABA/ALI, 1988).

14. Jean Harris, *Marking Time: Letters from Jean Harris to Shana Alexander* (New York: Charles Scriber's Sons, 1991), 142–145.

15. Ibid., 142–143.

16. *Shawshank Redemption* (Columbia Pictures, 1994).

17. Joseph Margulies, *Guantanamo and the Abuse of Presidential Power* (New York: Simon & Schuster, 2006), 138.

18. Kathleen M. Ridolfi, "Not Just an Act of Mercy: The Demise of Post-Conviction Relief and a Rightful Claim to Clemency," *New York Review of Law and Social Change* 24 (1998): 43.

19. Peter Marks, "Cuomo Grants Few NY Inmates a Holiday Break," *Newsday,* December 23, 1990, 7. One commentator noted that Cuomo's record of denials of clemency "ranks him among the least merciful governors." Colman McCarthy, "Cuomo's Small Favor to Jean Harris," *Washington Post,* January 9, 1993, A21.

20. Ellen Goodman, "Clemency for Prisoner 81-G–0098," *Boston Globe,* January 3, 1993, 71.

21. Nicholas Goldberg, "Crime: It's Cuomo's Albatross; But Record Belies Voters' View," *Newsday,* October 12, 1994, A4.

22. Wilbert Rideau, "Dying in Prison," in *Life Sentences: Rage and Survival Behind* Bars, ed. Wilbert Rideau and Ron Wikberg (New York: Times Books, 1992), 158, 159.

23. Raymond Hernandez, "Pataki Would Ease Drug Laws, but Ties Plan to Ending Parole," *New York Times,* May 4, 1999, A1.

Chapter 4, Freedom

1. Dorothy Allison, *Bastard Out of Carolina* (New York: E. P. Dutton, 1992).

2. "Number and Rate (per 100,000 resident population in each group) of Sentenced Prisoners Under Jurisdiction of State and Federal Correctional Authorities on Dec. 31, by Sex, United States, 1925–2004, Sourcebook of Criminal Justice Statistics Online," http://www .albany.edu/sourcebook/pdf/t6282004.pdf (last visited, Aug. 8, 2006).

As of June 30, 2005, there were 2,186,230 prisoners held in federal or state prisons or local jails. http://www.ojp.usdog.gov/bjs/prisons/htm (last visited, Aug. 3, 2006). For a thorough discussion of the policy of mass incarceration in the United States, see generally Marc Mauer, *Race to Incarcerate* (New York: The New Press, 1999).

3. Scott Christianson, *With Liberty for Some: 500 Years of Imprisonment in America* (Boston: Northeastern University Press, 1998).
4. Wendy Wasserstein, "My Mother, Then and Now," in *Bachelor Girls* (New York: Random House, 1992), 21.
5. Abbe Smith, "Rosie O'Neill Goes to Law School: The Clinical Education of a Sensitive, New Age Public Defender," *Harvard Civil Rights-Civil Liberties Law Review* 28 (1993): 36 (arguing that a lawyer is not a client's friend); but see Charles Fried, "The Lawyer as Friend: The Moral Foundations of the Lawyer-Client Relation," *Yale Law Journal* 85 (1976): 1060 (arguing that a lawyer is a client's "legal friend").
6. Calvin Trillin, "Paris and His Sisters," *The New Yorker,* April 19, 1999, 62.

Epilogue

1. Stephen Bright, president and senior counsel, Southern Center for Human Rights, makes this observation in nearly each of his speeches about the death penalty.
2. Bryan Stevenson, professor of clinical law, NYU School of Law, and executive director, Equal Justice Initiative of Alabama, often makes this observation in his speeches about the death penalty.
3. David Luban, *Legal Ethics and Human Dignity* (Cambridge: Cambridge University Press, 2007).

Index